Off Target

The Conduct of the War
and Civilian Casualties in Iraq

Human Rights Watch

New York   Washington   London   Brussels

ISBN: 1564322939

Cover photo: © 2003 Bruno Stevens

Caption: Al-Hilla, April 2003. A father holds his son who was wounded and lost his right foot during the invasion by Coalition forces. The child lost four family members, including his mother, grandmother, brother, and sister.

Cover design by Rafael Jimenez

Addresses for Human Rights Watch

350 Fifth Avenue, 34th Floor, New York, NY 10118-3299
Tel: (212) 290-4700, Fax: (212) 736-1300, E-mail: hrwnyc@hrw.org

1630 Connecticut Avenue, N.W., Suite 500, Washington, DC 20009
Tel: (202) 612-4321, Fax: (202) 612-4333, E-mail: hrwdc@hrw.org

2nd Floor, 2-12 Pentonville Road London N1 9HF, UK
Tel: (44 20) 7713 1995, Fax: (44 20) 7713 1800, E-mail: hrwuk@hrw.org

15 Rue Van Campenhout, 1000 Brussels, Belgium
Tel: (32 2) 732-2009, Fax: (32 2) 732-0471, E-mail: hrwbe@hrw.org

Web Site Address: http://www.hrw.org

Listserv address: To receive Human Rights Watch news releases by email, subscribe to the HRW news listserv of your choice by visiting
http://hrw.org/act/subscribe-mlists/subscribe.htm

Human Rights Watch is dedicated to
protecting the human rights of people around the world.

We stand with victims and activists to prevent
discrimination, to uphold political freedom, to protect people from inhumane
conduct in wartime, and to bring offenders to justice.

We investigate and expose
human rights violations and hold abusers accountable.

We challenge governments and those who hold power to end abusive practices and
respect international human rights law.

We enlist the public and the international
community to support the cause of human rights for all.

HUMAN RIGHTS WATCH

Human Rights Watch conducts regular, systematic investigations of human rights abuses in some seventy countries around the world. Our reputation for timely, reliable disclosures has made us an essential source of information for those concerned with human rights. We address the human rights practices of governments of all political stripes, of all geopolitical alignments, and of all ethnic and religious persuasions. Human Rights Watch defends freedom of thought and expression, due process and equal protection of the law, and a vigorous civil society; we document and denounce murders, disappearances, torture, arbitrary imprisonment, discrimination, and other abuses of internationally recognized human rights. Our goal is to hold governments accountable if they transgress the rights of their people.

Human Rights Watch began in 1978 with the founding of its Europe and Central Asia division (then known as Helsinki Watch). Today, it also includes divisions covering Africa, the Americas, Asia, and the Middle East. In addition, it includes three thematic divisions on arms, children's rights, and women's rights. It maintains offices in New York, Washington, Los Angeles, London, Brussels, Moscow, Tashkent, Tblisi, and Bangkok. Human Rights Watch is an independent, nongovernmental organization, supported by contributions from private individuals and foundations worldwide. It accepts no government funds, directly or indirectly.

The staff includes Kenneth Roth, executive director; Allison Adoradio, operations director, Michele Alexander, development director; Carroll Bogert, associate director; Steve Crawshaw, London office director, Barbara Guglielmo, finance director; Lotte Leicht, Brussels office director; Maria Pignataro Nielsen, human resources director; Iain Levine, program director; Rory Mungoven, advocacy director; Wilder Tayler, legal and policy director; and Joanna Weschler, United Nations representative.

The regional division directors of Human Rights Watch are Peter Takirambudde, Africa; José Miguel Vivanco, Americas; Brad Adams, Asia. The thematic division directors are Steve Goose, Arms; Lois Whitman, Children's Rights; and LaShawn R. Jefferson, Women's Rights. The program directors are Arvind Ganesan, Business and Human Rights; Joanne Csete, HIV/AIDS and Human Rights; Richard Dicker, International Justice; and Jamie Fellner, U.S. Program.

The members of the board of directors are Jonathan Fanton, Chair; Robert L. Bernstein, Founding Chair, Khaled Abou El Fadl, Lisa Anderson, Lloyd Axworthy, David Brown, William Carmichael, Jorge Castañeda, Dorothy Cullman, Edith Everett, Michael Gellert, Vartan Gregorian, James F. Hoge, Jr., Stephen L. Kass, Marina Pinto Kaufman, Wendy Keys, Robert Kissane, Bruce Klatsky, Joanne Leedom-Ackerman, Josh Mailman, Kati Marton, Barry Meyer, Joel Motley, Samuel K. Murumba, Jane Olson, Peter Osnos, Kathleen Peratis, Catherine Powell, Sigrid Rausing, Victoria Riskin, Orville Schell, Sid Sheinberg, Gary G. Sick, Domna Stanton, John J. Studzinski, Shibley Telhami, and Maya Wiley. Emeritus Board: Roland Algrant, Adrian DeWind, Alice H. Henkin, Bruce Rabb, and Malcolm Smith.

Off Target
The Conduct of the War and Civilian Casualties in Iraq

ACRONYMS

ATACMS	Army Tactical Missile System
BDA	Battle Damage Assessment
BLU	Bomb Live Unit
CBU	Cluster Bomb Unit
CCW	Convention on Conventional Weapons
CDE	Collateral Damage Estimate
CENTCOM	U.S. Central Command
CEP	Circular Error Probable
CIA	Central Intelligence Agency
CFLCC	Combined Forces Land Component Commander
CMOC	Civil-Military Operations Center
DGS	Directorate of General Security
DPICM	Dual-Purpose Improved Conventional Munition
EOD	Explosive Ordnance Disposal
ERW	Explosive Remnants of War
GIS	Geographic Information Software
GPS	Global Positioning System
HOC	Humanitarian Operations Center
ICRC	International Committee of the Red Cross
IHL	International Humanitarian Law
JAG	Judge Advocate General
JDAM	Joint Direct Attack Munition
JSOW	Joint Stand Off Weapon
MLRS	Multiple Launch Rocket System
NGO	Nongovernmental Organization
PGM	Precision-Guided Munition
PID	Positive Identification
ROE	Rules of Engagement
RPG	Rocket-Propelled Grenade
SADARM	Sense and Destroy Armor Munition
SEAD	Suppression of Enemy Air Defense
TLAM	Tomahawk Land Attack Missile
TST	Time-Sensitive Target
UAV	Unmanned Aerial Vehicle
UNMACT	U.N. Mine Action Coordination Team
UXO	Unexploded Ordnance
WCMD	Wind Corrected Munitions Dispenser

GLOSSARY

Abandoned Explosive Ordnance – Explosive ordnance that has not been used during a conflict and has been left behind unprotected or dumped by a party to an armed conflict. Abandoned explosive ordnance may or may not have been primed, fuzed, armed, or otherwise prepared for use.[*]

Battle Damage Assessment (BDA) – The timely and accurate estimate of damage resulting from the application of military force, either lethal or non-lethal, against a predetermined objective. Battle damage assessment can be applied to the employment of all types of weapon systems (air, ground, naval, and special forces weapon systems) throughout the range of military operations. Battle damage assessment is primarily an intelligence responsibility with required inputs and coordination from the operators. Battle damage assessment is composed of physical damage assessment, functional damage assessment, and target system assessment.[†] In the context of this report, battle damage assessment also refers to Human Rights Watch's assessment of the conduct of a war through the lens of international humanitarian law and the effects of a war on the civilian population.

Circular Error Probable (CEP) – An indicator of the delivery accuracy of a weapon system, used as a factor in determining probable damage to a target. It is the radius of a circle within which half of a missile's projectiles are expected to fall.[†]

Cluster Bomb Unit (CBU) – An aircraft store composed of a dispenser and submunitions.[†] Commonly known as a cluster bomb, the cluster bomb unit, which is an area effect weapon, is a single air-dropped bomb which ejects small bomblets, also called submunitions. They may explode on contact with the ground or be fuzed with a delay.

Collateral Damage Estimate (CDE) – Estimate of unintentional or incidental injury or damage to persons or objects that would not be lawful military targets in the circumstances ruling at the time. Such damage is not unlawful so long as it is not excessive in light of the overall military advantage anticipated from the attack. [†]

Dual-Purpose Improved Conventional Munition (DPICM) – U.S. Army and Marine Corps submunition that can be launched by artillery, often 155mm, or MLRS rocket. Also called a grenade, it has both anti-armor and antipersonnel effects.

Dud – Common term for unexploded munition or cluster submunition; refers to munitions or submunitions that have been fired but did not explode on impact as intended. These are often hazardous duds that can still explode when disturbed.

Emerging Target – A target that develops as the war progresses instead of being planned prior to the initiation of hostilities. Emerging targets include time-sensitive targets that are fleeting in nature (such as leadership), enemy forces in the field, mobile targets, and other targets of opportunity.

Explosive Remnants of War (ERW) – All types of unexploded ordnance as well as abandoned explosive ordnance.*

Global Positioning System (GPS) – A satellite constellation that provides highly accurate position, velocity, and time navigation information to users.†

High-Value Target – A target the enemy commander requires for the successful completion of the mission. The loss of high-value targets would be expected to seriously degrade important enemy functions throughout the friendly commander's area of interest.† In this report, it refers to Iraqi leadership targets.

Multiple Launch Rocket System (MLRS) – This rocket artillery system can carry up to twelve rockets, which can be launched simultaneously or individually. Each rocket contains 644 M77 submunitions.

Precision-Guided Munition (PGM) – A weapon that uses a computerized guidance system that directs it toward a target with increased accuracy and less collateral damage. GPS, laser, and television guidance systems are particularly common.

Rules of Engagement (ROE) – Directives issued by competent military authority that delineate the circumstances and limitations under which U.S. forces will initiate and/or continue combat engagement with other forces encountered.†

Thuraya – Satellite telephone company owned and operated in Abu Dhabi, United Arab Emirates. The Thuraya satellite phone is common in the Middle East. Thuraya phones have an internal GPS chip that allows tracking within a one-hundred-meter radius.

Time-Sensitive Target – Those targets requiring immediate response because they pose (or will soon pose) a danger to friendly forces or are highly lucrative, fleeting targets of opportunity.†

U.S. Central Command (CENTCOM) – One of nine Unified Combatant Commands assigned operational control of U.S. combat forces. Organized as a headquarters element, CENTCOM has no permanent fighting forces assigned to it; instead all four branches of the armed forces provide component commands to Central Command. Its area of responsibility extends from the Horn of Africa to Central Asia.‡

Unexploded Ordnance (UXO) – Explosive ordnance that has been primed, fuzed, armed, or otherwise prepared for use and used in an armed conflict. It may have been fired, dropped, launched, or projected and should have exploded but failed to do so.*

Wind Corrected Munitions Dispenser (WCMD) – Guidance kit for weapons which, using only inertial guidance, allows for drop from medium to high altitudes with corrections for wind effects and errors during drop. This kit is used on some models of cluster bombs, including the CBU-103 and the CBU-105.

---

* Convention on Conventional Weapons (CCW), Draft Explosive Remnants of War Protocol, September 2003.

† U.S. Department of Defense, "Dictionary of Military Terms," June 5, 2003, http://www.dtic.mil/doctrine/jel/doddict (retrieved October 21, 2003).

‡ U.S. Central Command, "About CENTCOM," n.d., http://www.centcom.mil/aboutus/centcom.htm (retrieved November 20, 2003).

I. SUMMARY AND RECOMMENDATIONS

Principal Findings

U.S. President George W. Bush called the war in Iraq "one of the swiftest and most humane military campaigns in history."[1] Yet thousands of Iraqi civilians were killed or injured during the three weeks of fighting from the first air strikes on March 20 to April 9, 2003, when Baghdad fell to U.S.-led Coalition forces.

Human Rights Watch conducted a mission to Iraq between late April and early June 2003 with two objectives: (1) to identify and investigate potential violations of international humanitarian law (IHL) by the parties to the conflict, and (2) to identify patterns of combat by those parties which may have caused civilian casualties and suffering that could have been avoided if additional precautions had been taken.

Human Rights Watch did not undertake this mission to determine the number of civilian casualties. Rather, it sought to understand how and why civilians were killed or injured in order to assess compliance with international humanitarian law, with a view to lessening the impact of war on civilians in the future.

The investigation showed that Iraqi forces committed a number of violations of international humanitarian law, which may have led to significant civilian casualties. These violations included use of human shields, abuse of the red cross and red crescent emblems, use of antipersonnel landmines, location of military objects in protected places (such as mosques, hospitals, and cultural property), and a failure to take adequate precautions to protect civilians from the dangers of military operations. The Iraqi military's practice of wearing civilian clothes tended to erode the distinction between combatants and civilians, putting the latter at risk, although it did not relieve Coalition forces of their obligation to distinguish at all times between combatants and civilians and to target only combatants.

U.S.-led Coalition forces took precautions to spare civilians and, for the most part, made efforts to uphold their legal obligations. Human Rights Watch nevertheless identified practices that led to civilian casualties in the air war, ground war, and post-conflict period.

---

[1] President George W. Bush, Address of the President to the Nation, September 7, 2003, http://www.whitehouse.gov/news/releases/2003/09/20030907-1.html (retrieved November 5, 2003).

The widespread use of cluster munitions, especially by U.S. and U.K. ground forces, caused at least hundreds of civilian casualties. Cluster munitions, which are large weapons containing dozens or hundreds of submunitions, endanger civilians because of their broad dispersal, or "footprint," and the high number of submunitions that do not explode on impact. U.S. Central Command (CENTCOM) reported that it used 10,782 cluster munitions,[2] which could contain at least 1.8 million submunitions. The British used an additional seventy air-launched and 2,100 ground-launched cluster munitions, containing 113,190 submunitions. Although cluster munition strikes are particularly dangerous in populated areas, U.S. and U.K. ground forces repeatedly used these weapons in attacks on Iraqi positions in residential neighborhoods. Coalition air forces also caused civilian casualties by their use of cluster munitions, but to a much lesser degree.

Many of the civilian casualties from the air war occurred during U.S. attacks targeting senior Iraqi leaders. The United States used an unsound targeting methodology that relied on intercepts of satellite phones and inadequate corroborating intelligence. Thuraya satellite phones provide geo-coordinates that are accurate only to within a one-hundred-meter (328-foot) radius; therefore, the United States could not determine the origin of a call to a degree of accuracy greater than a 31,400-square-meter area. This flawed targeting strategy was compounded by a lack of effective assessment both prior to the attacks of the potential risks to civilians and after the attacks of their success and utility. All of the fifty acknowledged attacks targeting Iraqi leadership failed. While they did not kill a single targeted individual, the strikes killed and injured dozens of civilians. Iraqis who spoke to Human Rights Watch about the attacks it investigated repeatedly stated that they believed the intended targets were not even present at the time of the strikes.

Coalition air strikes on preplanned fixed targets apparently caused few civilian casualties, and U.S. and U.K. air forces generally avoided civilian infrastructure. Coalition forces did, however, identify certain targets as "dual use," including electricity and media installations. Human Rights Watch's investigations found that air strikes on civilian power distribution facilities in al-Nasiriyya caused serious civilian suffering and that the legality of the attacks on media installations was questionable.

---

[2] U.S. CENTCOM, executive summary of report on cluster munitions, 2003, provided to Human Rights Watch by Paul Wiseman, *USA Today*.

Most of the civilian casualties attributable to Coalition conduct in the ground war appear to have been the result of ground-launched cluster munitions. In some instances of direct combat, especially in Baghdad and al-Nasiriyya, problems with training on as well as dissemination and clarity of the rules of engagement (ROE) for U.S. ground forces may have contributed to loss of civilian life.

Explosive remnants of war (ERW) caused hundreds of civilian casualties during and after major hostilities and continue to do so today. The Coalition left behind many tens of thousands of cluster munition "duds," i.e. submunitions that did not explode on impact and which then became *de facto* landmines. If the average failure rate were 5 percent, the number of cluster munitions Coalition forces reported using would leave about 90,000 duds. The humanitarian and military harm they caused has led even some of the soldiers who fought in Iraq to call for an alternative to a weapon that produces so many duds. Meanwhile, Iraqi forces abandoned staggering quantities of arms and ammunition that have injured or killed civilians searching for playthings or scraps to sell or reuse.

U.S. and U.K. military and civilian leaders have repeatedly stressed their commitment to avoiding civilian casualties and other harm to civilians. Neither country, however, does an adequate job of investigating and analyzing why civilian casualties occur. That job, left largely to organizations like Human Rights Watch, should be the responsibility of parties to the conflict. Having the capability to do this kind of assessment, the United States and United Kingdom should accurately account for the civilian casualties they cause in armed conflict so that they can provide maximum protection to civilians in any future conflict.

International Humanitarian Law

During the war in Iraq, Coalition and Iraqi forces were bound by international humanitarian law, also known as the law of armed conflict. IHL requires parties to an armed conflict to respect and protect civilians and other persons not or no longer taking a direct part in hostilities. It also limits permissible means and methods of warfare. Especially relevant are the four Geneva Conventions of 1949, to which Iraq, the United States, and the United Kingdom are party.[3] Also applicable are the 1907 Hague

---

[3] Geneva Convention for the Amelioration of the Condition of the Wounded and Sick in Armed Forces in the Field of 12 August 1949 (First Geneva Convention), 75 U.N.T.S. 31, entered into force October 21, 1950; Geneva Convention for the Amelioration of the Condition of Wounded, Sick and Shipwrecked Members of Armed Forces at Sea of 12 August 1949 (Second Geneva Convention), 75 U.N.T.S. 85, entered into force October 21, 1950; Geneva Convention Relative to the Treatment of Prisoners of War of 12 August 1949 (Third Geneva Convention), 75 U.N.T.S. 135, entered into force October 21, 1950; Geneva Convention Relative to the

Regulations, ratified by the United States and the United Kingdom and widely accepted as representing customary international law.[4]

Neither Iraq nor the United States have ratified the First Additional Protocol of 1977 to the 1949 Geneva Conventions (Protocol I), though the United Kingdom is a party.[5] Protocol I codified and in some measure expanded upon existing law, particularly relating to the conduct of hostilities. Today, many, if not most, of its provisions are considered reflective of customary international law.[6]

The principle of distinction is the keystone of the law regulating conduct of hostilities. It requires parties to a conflict to distinguish at all times between combatants and civilians. Civilians and civilian objects may not be attacked, and operations may only be directed against military objectives.[7]

Military objectives are members of the armed forces, other persons taking a direct part in hostilities for the duration of their participation, and "those objects which by their

---

Protection of Civilian Persons in Time of War of 12 August 1949 (Fourth Geneva Convention), 75 U.N.T.S. 287, entered into force October 21, 1950.

[4] Convention (IV) Respecting the Laws and Customs of War on Land and the Annexed Regulations Concerning the Laws and Customs of War on Land of 18 October 1907 (Hague Regulations), 3 Martens Nouveau Recueil (ser. 3) 461, 187 Consol. T.S. 227, entered into force January 26, 1910.

[5] Protocol Additional to the Geneva Conventions of 12 August 1949, and Relating to the Protection of Victims of International Armed Conflicts (Protocol I) of 8 June 1977, 1125 U.N.T.S. 3, entered into force December 7, 1978.

[6] The U.S. military considers "evidence of the customary law of war arising from the general consent of States," as that which "may be found in judicial decisions, the writings of jurists, diplomatic correspondence, and other documentary material concerning the practice of States." U.S. Army Field Manual, FM 27-10, The Law of Land Warfare, July 18, 1956, art. 6. In 1987, then U.S. State Department Deputy Legal Advisor Michael Matheson publicly enumerated many of the principles enshrined in Protocol I that the United States considers customary international law. Among them are: limitations on the means and methods of warfare, especially those methods which cause superfluous injury or unnecessary suffering (art. 35); protection of the civilian population and individual citizens, as such, from being the object of acts or threats of violence, and from attacks that would clearly result in civilian casualties disproportionate to the expected military advantage (art. 51); protection of civilians from use as human shields (arts. 51 and 52); prohibition of the starvation of civilians as a method of warfare and allowing the delivery of impartial humanitarian aid necessary for the survival of the civilian population (arts. 54 and 70); taking into account military and humanitarian considerations in conducting military operations in order to minimize incidental death, injury, and damage to civilians and civilian objects, and providing advance warning to civilians unless circumstances do not permit (arts. 57-60). Michael J. Matheson, Remarks on the United States Position on the Relation of Customary International Law to the 1977 Protocols Additional to the 1949 Geneva Conventions, reprinted in "The Sixth Annual American Red-Cross Washington College of Law Conference on International Humanitarian Law: A Workshop on Customary International Law and the 1977 Protocols Additional to the 1949 Geneva Conventions," *American University Journal of International Law and Policy*, vol. 2, no. 2, Fall 1987, pp. 419-27.

[7] Protocol I, art. 48.

nature, location, purpose or use make an effective contribution to military action and whose total or partial destruction, capture or neutralization, in the circumstances ruling at the time, offers a definite military advantage."[8]

In addition to direct attacks against civilians, IHL also prohibits indiscriminate attacks. These are attacks "of a nature to strike military objectives and civilians or civilian objects without distinction."[9] Examples of indiscriminate attacks are those that "are not directed at a specific military objective" or that use means that "cannot be directed at a specific military objective."[10]

Also indiscriminate are attacks which violate the principle of proportionality because they are "expected to cause incidental loss of civilian life, injury to civilians [or] damage to civilian objectives . . . which would be excessive in relation to the concrete and direct military advantage anticipated" from that attack.[11]

In the conduct of military operations, constant care must be taken to spare the civilian population and civilian objects from the effects of hostilities. Parties to a conflict are therefore required to take precautionary measures with a view to avoiding, and in any event to minimizing, incidental loss of civilian life, injury to civilians, and damage to civilian objects. These precautions include:

- Doing "everything feasible to verify" that the objects to be attacked are military objectives and not civilians or civilian objects or subject to special protection.

- Taking "all feasible precautions in the choice of means and methods" of warfare so as to avoid and in any event minimize "incidental loss of civilian life, injury to civilians and damage to civilian objects."

- Refraining from launching attacks "expected to cause incidental loss of civilian life, injury to civilians, [or] damage to civilian objects . . . which would be excessive in relation to the concrete and direct military advantage expected."

- When circumstances permit, giving "effective advance warning . . . of attacks which may affect the civilian population."

____

[8] Ibid., arts. 51(3), 52.

[9] Ibid., art. 51(4).

[10] Ibid., art. 51(4)(a, b).

[11] Ibid., art. 51(5)(b).

- "When a choice is possible between several military objectives for obtaining the same military advantage," carrying out the attack that may be "expected to cause the least danger to civilian lives and civilian objects."

- Avoiding "locating military objectives within or near densely populated areas."

- Endeavoring "to remove the civilian population . . . from the vicinity of military objectives."[12]

Parties to a conflict are also prohibited from using civilians "to shield military objectives from attacks" or using their presence "to shield, favour or impede military operations."[13]

Medical establishments and cultural property benefit from special protection under international humanitarian law. Hospitals and other medical units must be "respected and protected" and must not be the object of attack. They must not be used "to shield military objectives from attack."[14] They lose this protection, however, if they are used to commit "acts harmful to the enemy."[15]

Parties to a conflict must also refrain from committing hostile acts against "historic monuments, works of art or places of worship which constitute the cultural or spiritual heritage of peoples . . . [or] to use such objects in support of military effort."[16]

Methodology

Human Rights Watch has conducted several battle damage assessment (BDA) missions in the past to investigate the conduct of war and civilian casualties, including in Yugoslavia in 1999 and Afghanistan in 2002. While the military conducts such assessments to determine the military success of an operation, Human Rights Watch reviews the same incidents from an IHL perspective. For this mission to Iraq, Human Rights Watch conducted its research in three phases: pre-mission, on mission, and post-mission.

---

[12] Protocol I, arts. 57, 58.

[13] Ibid., art. 51(7).

[14] Ibid., art. 12.

[15] Ibid., art. 13.

[16] Ibid., art. 53. See also the 1954 Convention for the Protection of Cultural Property in the Event of War, which has been ratified by Iraq.

Pre-Mission

During the active phase of hostilities, Human Rights Watch monitored press reports from around the world of civilians injured or killed by the fighting. It examined each report for the location, date, and time of the incident as well as the tactics and weapons employed and the military forces involved. The reports were compiled into an electronic database on a daily basis, which helped Human Rights Watch researchers to determine the initial sites for inspection and analysis inside Iraq. The pre-mission work also included the creation of ArcView geographic information software (GIS) customized maps of Iraq and its major cities. These digitized maps would be used to display data collected inside Iraq of the precise location of various objects and events.

On Mission

Human Rights Watch sent a team of three researchers to Iraq between April 29 and June 1, 2003, to investigate the effect of the air war, ground war, and the immediate post-combat environment on civilians. The team included a senior military analyst and Iraq expert, a lawyer with expertise in international humanitarian law and the use of cluster munitions, and a principal researcher. All three had previous experience with this kind of research.[17] The team focused on the main areas of fighting in the Tigris and Euphrates river valleys where civilian deaths were reported. Guided initially by their press report database and later by information they received from sources inside Iraq, the team visited ten cities, including Umm Qasr, al-Fao, Basra, al-Nasiriyya, al-Shatra, Baghdad, al-Hilla, Karbala', al-Najaf and al-Falluja. It obtained data about the location of cluster munition strikes from the Humanitarian Operations Center (HOC) in Kuwait, plotted those strikes in ArcView, and visited many of the sites located in populated areas. The team traveled freely both within and between cities by private vehicle, unarmed and without military escort.

At each of the sites visited, the team attempted to investigate three sources of information: ballistics, belligerents, and the victims.

- *Ballistics*: Ballistic evidence included blast and fragmentation damage and, especially in the case of cluster munitions, pieces of weapons; this information helped the team

---

[17] Before coming to Human Rights Watch, Senior Military Analyst Marc Garlasco worked as an intelligence officer on Iraq in the U.S. Defense Intelligence Agency. He did a battle damage assessment for the Pentagon in Kosovo. All the findings in this report are based on work he did after joining Human Rights Watch. Bonnie Docherty, lawyer and researcher, and Reuben E. Brigety, II, former researcher, conducted a battle damage assessment for Human Rights Watch in Afghanistan in March 2002.

determine the weapons used in a particular incident and the manner in which they were employed.

- *Belligerents*: The team attempted to interview soldiers from all parties to an incident who could provide information about how they fought particular engagements, including details on the weapons and tactics they used, the behavior they observed from the enemy, and the presence of civilians at the time of the attack.

- *Victims*: The team interviewed victims and witnesses of attacks that harmed civilians to gather information about the time, date, location, and nature of incidents. They also reviewed thousands of medical records at more than a dozen hospitals in the cities they visited and interviewed medical personnel at those facilities.

In addition, at each site, the team recorded the precise global positioning system (GPS) coordinates of important locations—such as debris fields, bomb craters, shrapnel and small-arms damage, location of Coalition and Iraqi forces according to witness testimony, places of civilian deaths or injuries—with hand-held Garmin GPS units. The team also took thousands of digital photographs to analyze in conjunction with the evidence described above.

It must be stressed that, with one exception, Human Rights Watch was unable to interview members of the Iraqi armed forces in order to get their response to accusations of violations of IHL and their views on how the Coalition forces fought. This report does not assess the military advantage of any particular attack it describes. Parties to an armed conflict must carry out this assessment on a case-by-case basis before each attack.

Post-Mission

After returning from Iraq, the team compiled and analyzed all of the information it gathered during the mission. It also conducted follow-up interviews with relevant U.S. and U.K. officials.

Civilian Casualties

Human Rights Watch did not attempt to quantify civilian deaths in Iraq. Although an overall number would be useful in order to understand fully the impact of the war and to perform comparative analyses with other recent conflicts, we believe it is more important to understand the circumstances that led to civilian casualties.

Human Rights Watch researchers went to many of the hospitals in the ten cities and numerous small towns they visited during the mission. Hospital directors and medical personnel who had been working in these facilities during the conflict made Iraqi medical records available.[18] These records allowed the researchers to draw some statistical conclusions, but they also highlighted the challenges in attempting an accurate count of civilian casualties.

The quality of the records varied from detailed computerized hospital forms to bloodstained notebooks with hand-written notes. While some medical facilities were able to keep comprehensive records, others had incomplete records with sections missing. Understandably, during active military operations, record keeping was not always the highest priority. This is one reason that the total number of civilian casualties in Iraq will never be accurately known. Another challenge to quantifying Iraqi civilian casualties is that in this Muslim nation the dead are buried almost immediately. Though hospitals have records of some of the deaths in the war, a certain percentage of casualties, due to religious customs, were not taken to hospitals, not even to obtain death certificates. Finally, as in any war, in some instances, there were few if any remains by which to identify the dead.

Though a complete accounting of civilian casualties may not be possible, some attempts to quantify the dead have been made. The Associated Press canvassed sixty of Iraq's 124 hospitals immediately after the end of major combat operations and calculated that at least 3,420 civilians died. The Associated Press described the count as "fragmentary" and said, "the complete toll—if it is ever tallied—is sure to be significantly higher."[19] The *Los Angeles Times* did a survey of twenty-seven hospitals in Baghdad and outlying areas and found that at least 1,700 civilians died and more than 8,000 were injured in the capital.[20]

Statistics drawn from hospital records indicate that the ground war caused the vast majority of the deaths. More than 400 civilians died in al-Nasiriyya, including at least 72 women and 169 children; more than 700 additional women and children were injured. The preponderance of these casualties was due to small arms fire as the battle raged in a densely populated neighborhood of the city. Baghdad had similarly high casualties from ground fire. In al-Hilla, U.S. ground-launched cluster munitions caused 90 percent of all

---

[18] See appendices on civilian casualties in al-Hilla, al-Najaf, and al-Nasiriyya.

[19] Niko Price "3,240 Civilian Deaths in Iraq," Associated Press, June 10, 2003.

[20] Laura King, "Baghdad's Death Toll Assessed," *Los Angeles Times*, May 18, 2003.

civilian casualties. These weapons killed large numbers of civilians in Basra and Baghdad as well. While the ground war caused significantly more casualties, the air war, especially failed attacks targeting Iraqi leadership, contributed to the total number of civilian deaths and injuries.

`Ali Kadhim Hashim stands in front of the rubble where his family was killed in a U.S. Marine helicopter attack in al-Nasiriyya. Fourteen members of his family died in the home on March 23, 2003, including his parents, his wife, and his children. © 2003 Reuben E. Brigety, II / Human Rights Watch

Major Recommendations

Human Rights Watch makes the following major recommendations to the United States, the United Kingdom, and other Coalition forces:

- Air attacks on leadership targets, like those launched in Iraq, should not be carried out until the intelligence and targeting failures have been corrected. Leadership strikes should not be carried out without an adequate collateral damage estimate (CDE); strikes should not be based solely on satellite phone intercepts; and there should be no strikes in densely populated areas unless the intelligence is considered highly reliable.

- A thorough investigation of the collateral damage and battle damage assessment processes should be carried out to determine how they can be improved to reduce civilian casualties, and appropriate changes should be implemented.

- There should be no use of air- or ground-delivered cluster munitions until the humanitarian problems associated with these weapons are resolved. In particular, their use should be suspended until the dud rate can be reduced dramatically. If cluster munitions are employed, they should not be used in or near populated areas. Stocks of older, highly unreliable and unguided cluster bombs should not be used under any circumstances.

- Precision-guided munitions (PGMs) should be used whenever possible, especially on targets in populated areas.

- Extreme caution must be used in the targeting of electrical power facilities. In particular, electrical generation facilities should not be attacked at all. If electrical distribution facilities are attacked, it should be done in such a way as to cause only temporarily incapacitation.

- Media installations should not be attacked unless it is clear that they make an effective contribution to military action and their destruction offers a definite military advantage.

- Armed forces should conduct better training on the application of rules of engagement, especially in urban warfare and in circumstances where the enemy may be wearing civilian clothes. The U.S. military should ensure that there is no confusion between written and verbal rules of engagement and that ROE are distributed in a timely fashion.

- More planning, personnel, and resources need to be devoted to dealing with unexploded ordnance and abandoned stockpiles of arms and ammunition both during conflict and immediately afterward.

II. CONDUCT OF THE AIR WAR

Significant civilian casualties occurred in the air war in Iraq despite the use of a high percentage of precision weapons. Of the 29,199 bombs dropped during the war by the United States and United Kingdom, nearly two-thirds (19,040) were precision-guided munitions.[21] In the Persian Gulf conflict in 1991, 8 percent of all bombs dropped were PGMs; in Yugoslavia in 1999 approximately one-third were PGMs; in Afghanistan in 2002 approximately 65 percent were PGMs.[22]

Many of the civilian casualties from the air war occurred during U.S. attacks targeting senior Iraqi leaders. The United States used an unsound targeting methodology that relied on intercepts of satellite phones and inadequate corroborating intelligence. Targeting based on geo-coordinates derived from satellite phones in essence rendered U.S. precision weapons potentially indiscriminate. This flawed targeting strategy was compounded by the lack of an effective assessment both prior to the attacks of the risks to civilians (what the U.S. military calls a "collateral damage estimate" or CDE) and following the attacks of their success and utility (what the U.S. military calls a "battle damage assessment" or BDA).

The use of air-delivered cluster bombs against targets in or near populated areas also contributed to the civilian death toll, although to a lesser degree. As detailed in the ground war chapter of this report, ground-delivered cluster munitions were a major cause of civilian casualties, while air-delivered cluster weapons caused a relatively small number of civilian casualties.

Beyond serious technical or human failures resulting in missed targets, largely avoided in Iraq were the types of attacks that led to significant civilian casualties and civilian suffering in previous U.S. air wars: extensive use of cluster bombs in or near populated

---

[21] Lieutenant General T. Michael Moseley, U.S. Air Force, "Operation Iraqi Freedom—By The Numbers," April 30, 2003, p. 11 [hereinafter "Operation Iraqi Freedom—By The Numbers"]. This report cites a total of 19,948 guided weapons, including guided cluster bombs, but guided cluster bombs cannot be considered precision weapons because of their large dispersal area. In terms of raw numbers, 1,263 more PGMs were dropped in the first Gulf War than in the 2003 Iraq war. General Accounting Office, "Operation Desert Storm: Evaluation of the Air Campaign," GAO/NSIAD-97-134, June 1997, appendix 4, table IV.4 (Unit Cost and Expenditure of Selected Guided and Unguided Munitions in Desert Storm).

[22] Herman L. Gilster, "Desert Storm: War, Time, and Substitution Revisited," *Airpower*, Spring 1996, p. 8; Michael Kelly, "The American Way of War," *Atlantic Monthly*, June 2002, p. 16; Gerry Gilmore, "Crusader Not 'Truly Transformational,' Rumsfeld Says," American Forces Press Services, May 16, 2002.

areas; destruction of electrical and other dual-use facilities; widespread daylight attacks; and inappropriate targeting choices, particularly with respect to mobile targets.

Coalition forces took significant steps to protect civilians during the air war, including increased use of precision-guided munitions when attacking targets situated in populated areas and generally careful target selection. The United States and United Kingdom recognized that employment of precision-guided munitions alone was not enough to provide civilians with adequate protection. They employed other methods to help minimize civilian casualties, such as bombing at night when civilians were less likely to be on the streets, using penetrator munitions and delayed fuzes to ensure that most blast and fragmentation damage was kept within the impact area, and using attack angles that took into account the locations of civilian facilities such as schools and hospitals.[23]

But there were still failures in the conduct of the air war that led to the loss of civilian life or to other civilian harm. The most egregious was the flawed targeting of Iraqi leadership. While to a lesser extent than in other recent conflicts, U.S. and U.K. air forces also used some cluster bombs in or near populated areas. Attacks on certain civilian power facilities caused additional civilian suffering, and the legality of attacks on media installations was questionable.

This section contains a synopsis of the air war, an examination of attacks on Iraqi leadership and other emerging targets (including problems related to collateral damage estimates and battle damage assessment), and an analysis of attacks on fixed strategic targets (including electrical power, telecommunications, media, and government and military facilities). Finally, it looks at the problematic use of air-delivered cluster bombs by the United States and the United Kingdom.

Synopsis of the Air War

The war in Iraq started at 3:15 a.m. on March 20, 2003, with an attempt to "decapitate" the Iraqi leadership by killing Saddam Hussein.[24] This unsuccessful air strike was not

---

[23] See Human Rights Watch telephone interview with senior CENTCOM official #1, Tampa, September 27, 2003.

[24] A useful timeline of the war was published in *The Guardian* and is available at www.guardian.co.uk. All dates and times in this section are local Iraq times.

part of long-term planning but was instead a "target of opportunity" based on late-breaking intelligence, which ultimately proved incorrect.[25]

The major air war effort began at approximately 6:00 p.m. on the same day with an aerial bombardment of Baghdad and the Iraqi integrated air defense system. During the early morning hours of March 21, Coalition air forces attacked targets in Basra, Mosul, al-Hilla, and elsewhere in Iraq. On the night of March 21, precision-guided munitions began destroying government facilities in the Iraqi capital. The air war shifted to attacks on Republican Guard divisions south of Baghdad after the sandstorms of March 25 stalled the ground offensive, but the bombardment of Baghdad continued. U.S. forces hit telecommunications facilities on the night of March 27.

Daylight bombing in Baghdad began on March 31, and elements of the Republican Guard around the city bore the brunt of the aerial assault aimed at paving the way for U.S. ground forces. The bombing of government facilities largely ceased by the morning of April 3 when the airport was taken, but attacks on Republican Guard units continued. On April 5, close air support missions flew over Baghdad to support ground combat. The same day, the United States bombed the reported safe house of `Ali Hassan al-Majid (known as "Chemical Ali") in Basra. On April 7, air attacks targeted Saddam Hussein and other Iraqi leaders in Baghdad. On April 9, Baghdad fell.

Collateral Damage Estimates

The U.S. military uses the term "collateral damage" when referring to harm to civilians and civilian structures from an attack on a military target. Collateral damage estimates are part of the U.S. military's official targeting process and are usually prepared for targets well in advance.[26] Since the CDE influences target selection, weapon selection, and even time and angle of attack, it is the military's best means of minimizing civilian casualties and other losses in air strikes.

Collateral damage assessments are a key way for the military to fulfill its obligations under international humanitarian law. International humanitarian law requires an attack to be cancelled or suspended if it is expected to cause loss of civilian life or property that "would be excessive in relation to the concrete and direct military advantage

---

[25] Technical Sergeant Mark Kinkade, "The First Shot," *Airman*, July 23, 2003, http://www.af.mil/news/airman/0703/air.html (retrieved November 13, 2003).

[26] "Targeting and Collateral Damage," U.S. CENTCOM Briefing, March 5, 2003.

anticipated."[27] Assessment of collateral damage is necessary to perform this proportionality test adequately.

U.S. air forces carry out a collateral damage estimate using a computer model designed to determine the weapon, fuze, attack angle, and time of day that will ensure maximum effect on a target with minimum civilian casualties.[28] Defense Secretary Donald Rumsfeld reportedly had to authorize personally all targets that had a collateral damage estimate of more than thirty civilian casualties.[29]

Asked how carefully the U.S. Air Force reviewed strikes in Iraq for collateral damage, a senior U.S. Central Command official responded, "with excruciating pain." He told Human Rights Watch,

> [T]he primary concern for the conduct of the war was to do it with absolutely minimum civilian casualties. . . . The first concern is having the desired effect on a target. . . . Next is to use the minimum weapon to achieve that effect. In the process, collateral damage may become one of the considerations that would affect what weapon we had to choose. . . . All of the preplanned targets had a CDE done very early in the process, many months before the war was actually fought. . . . For emerging target strikes, we still do a CDE, but do it very quickly. The computer software was able to rapidly model collateral effects.[30]

Strikes with high collateral damage estimates received extra review. According to another senior CENTCOM official,

> CENTCOM came up with a list of twenty-four to twenty-eight high CDE targets that we were concerned about. . . . They had a direct relationship to command and control of Iraqi military forces. These [high CDE targets] were briefed all the way to Bush. He understood the targets, what their use was, and that even under optimum circumstances, there would still be as many as X number of civilian casualties. This was

---

[27] Protocol I, art. 57(2)(b).

[28] Human Rights Watch telephone interview with senior CENTCOM official #1.

[29] Bradley Graham, "U.S. Moved Early for Air Supremacy," *Washington Post*, July 20, 2003, p. A26.

[30] Human Rights Watch telephone interview with senior CENTCOM official #1.

> the high CD target list. There were originally over 11,000 aim points
> when we started the high collateral targeting. Many were thrown out,
> many were mitigated. We hit twenty of these high collateral damage
> targets.[31]

Strikes against emerging targets also received review although the process was done much more quickly. U.S. Army Major General Stanley McChrystal, vice director for operations on the Joint Chiefs of Staff, explained the situation in this way:

> There tends to be a careful process where there is plenty of time to
> review that [the targets]. . . . [T]hen we put together certain processes
> like time-sensitive targeting. And those are when you talk about the
> crush of an emerging target that might come up, that doesn't have time
> to go through a complicated vetting process. . . . [T]here still is a legal
> review, but it is all at a much accelerated process because there are some
> fleeting targets that require a very time-sensitive engagement, but they all
> fit into pre-thought out criteria.[32]

For the most part, the collateral damage assessment process for the air war in Iraq worked well, especially with respect to preplanned targets. Human Rights Watch's month-long investigation in Iraq found that, in most cases, aerial bombardment resulted in minimal adverse effects to the civilian population.

The major exception was emerging targets, especially leadership targets. A Department of Defense source told Human Rights Watch that CENTCOM did not perform adequate collateral damage estimates for all of the leadership strikes due to perceived time constraints.[33] While the U.S. military hailed the quick turn-around time between the acquisition of intelligence and the air strikes on leadership targets, it appears the haste contributed to excessive civilian casualties because it prevented adequate collateral damage estimates.

---

[31] Human Rights Watch telephone interview with senior CENTCOM official #2, Tampa, September 27, 2003.

[32] Major General Stanley McChrystal, "Coalition Targeting Procedures," Foreign Press Center Briefing, April 3, 2003.

[33] Human Rights Watch interview with Department of Defense official, Washington, D.C., August 2003.

Emerging Targets—Iraqi Leadership

Emerging targets develop as a war progresses instead of being planned prior to the initiation of hostilities. They include time-sensitive targets (TSTs) that are fleeting in nature (such as leadership), enemy forces in the field, mobile targets, and other targets of opportunity.

It appears that U.S. air forces learned some lessons from the problems encountered with emerging targets in recent conflicts. Perhaps most notably, in Yugoslavia, U.S. aircraft bombed many civilian convoys after mistaking them for military targets.[34] In Iraq, there was only one reported case of a civilian vehicle being mistakenly targeted by aircraft.[35] Human Rights Watch researchers also found no instances of civilian casualties directly related to air strikes against Iraqi forces in the field, except those involving use of cluster bombs.[36]

A significant new problem related to emerging targets, however, was evident in Iraq. The targeting of Iraqi leadership resulted in dozens of civilian casualties that the United States could have prevented if it had taken additional precautions. This phenomenon has gone largely unremarked upon by U.S. military and civilian officials.

The United States targeted adversary leadership in prior armed conflicts. It did so in a limited way in Yugoslavia when Slobodan Milosevic's residence was bombed in an attempt to kill him.[37] The effort was more widespread in Afghanistan. As part of the

---

[34] See, for example, Human Rights Watch, "Civilian Deaths in the NATO Air Campaign," *A Human Rights Watch Report*, vol. 12, no. 1 (D), February 2000. This report identifies seven attacks on civilian convoys. There were other problematic attacks on emerging targets in Yugoslavia and Afghanistan. See "Afghanistan Civilian Deaths Mount," BBC News Online, January 3, 2002, http://news.bbc.co.uk/1/hi/world/south_asia/1740538.stm (retrieved October 21, 2003).

[35] On March 24, 2003, a U.S. warplane attacking a bridge about one hundred miles (160 kilometers) from the border with Syria accidentally bombed a bus crossing the bridge, according to Major General McChrystal. Syria claimed five civilians were killed and ten injured. "Civilians Killed in Northern Air Assault," Australian Broadcasting Corporation News Online, March 25, 2003, http://www.abc.net.au/news/newsitems/s815316.htm (retrieved October 20, 2003); "Syria Says Bus Carrying Civilians Bombed by Coalition Plane," PBS Online NewsHour, March 24, 2003, http://www.pbs.org/newshour/updates/syria_03-24-03.html (retrieved October 20, 2003).

[36] Destroyed Iraqi military vehicles litter the Iraqi countryside. Many were destroyed by air strikes before U.S. ground forces were anywhere near them. During an interview, Colonel David Perkins, commanding officer of the Second Brigade, Third Infantry Division, stated that precision-guided bombs hit many Iraqi vehicles long before his forces encountered them. Later, when scout units found Iraqi forces, U.S. ground forces would often call in air strikes instead of engaging with them with direct fire. Human Rights Watch interview with Colonel David Perkins, commanding officer, Second Brigade, Third Infantry Division, U.S. Army, Baghdad, May 23, 2003.

[37] Bradley Graham, "Missiles Hit State TV, Residence of Milosevic," *Washington Post*, April 23, 1999.

attempt to kill Taliban leader Mullah Omar and al-Qaeda head Osama bin Laden, the United States bombed homes associated with the two men. It also attacked convoys and destroyed caves in the pursuit of Taliban and al-Qaeda leadership.[38] Afghanistan, however, has few population centers, and most attacks occurred in relatively remote areas. In Iraq, by contrast, U.S. planes bombed densely populated neighborhoods in their attacks on Iraqi leadership.

The aerial strikes on Iraqi leadership constituted one of the most disturbing aspects of the war in Iraq for several reasons. First, many of the civilian casualties from the air war occurred during U.S. attacks on senior Iraqi leadership officials. Second, the intelligence and targeting methodologies used to identify potential leadership targets were inherently flawed and led to preventable civilian deaths. Finally, every single attack on leadership failed. None of the targeted individuals was killed, and in the cases examined by Human Rights Watch, local Iraqis repeatedly stated that they believed the intended targets were not even present at the time of the strike.

Time-Sensitive and High-Value Targets

During the war in Iraq, the U.S. Central Command identified a set of emerging targets as "time sensitive." Time-sensitive targets were targets that were fleeting in nature.[39] According to a senior official, CENTCOM designated leadership targets, a subset of time-sensitive targets, as high-value targets due to their perceived intrinsic value to the successful conclusion of major combat operations.[40]

The high-value targets included the top fifty-five Iraqis on the "Black List" of the Central Intelligence Agency (CIA). This became CENTCOM's "most wanted" list.[41] In total, the United States launched fifty attacks against Iraqi leaders in rapidly planned and executed air strikes. By mid-November 2003, forty of the fifty-five had been captured or killed or had surrendered—all after the declared end of major combat operations. The remaining fifteen, including Saddam Hussein, are considered "at large" by CENTCOM.[42]

---

[38] "U.S. Official Says Bin Laden Running Out of Options," *Los Angeles Times*, December 11, 2001.

[39] "Operation Iraqi Freedom—By The Numbers," p. 9. This document identifies three types of TSTs: leadership, weapons of mass destruction, and terrorists. It states there were 102 attacks on weapons of mass destruction, fifty on leadership, and four on terrorists. Ibid.

[40] Human Rights Watch telephone interview with senior CENTCOM official #2.

[41] Ibid.

[42] For the status of the fifty-five most wanted, see U.S. CENTCOM, "Iraqi 55 Most Wanted List," n.d., http://www.centcom.mil/Operations/Iraqi_Freedom/55mostwanted.htm (retrieved October 20, 2003).

Of the fifty aerial strikes against Iraqi leaders, not one resulted in the death of the intended target. Yet in four strikes researched by Human Rights Watch, forty-two civilians were killed and dozens more were injured. Human Rights Watch investigated other air strikes resulting in civilian casualties that appear to have been attacks targeting leadership, but it has been unable to confirm the identity of the intended target.[43]

The dismal record in targeting leadership is not unique to the war in Iraq. Apparently, in both Yugoslavia and Afghanistan, not one of the intended leadership targets was killed in an air strike.[44] In fact, the United States in the past has admitted it did not even know at whom it was shooting. Following a November 2001 attack on a suspected leadership target in Afghanistan, Pentagon spokesperson Victoria Clarke stated, "This was a good target. They had a confluence of intelligence which led us to believe there was senior leadership in the building. We don't have names. We don't have a sense of exactly who was in there."[45] It is difficult to understand how the military could assess a "good target" if it admits not knowing who the target was.

In an August 2003 report, the U.S. Air Force criticized its use of time-sensitive targeting in Afghanistan. Although it had targeted leadership in previous conflicts, the United States introduced the TST process in Afghanistan as it fused highly accurate weapons with the ability to target in near-real time. The report found that a "single authoritative TST process doctrine does not exist" and that "[t]here is no mechanism to measure performance of TST processes."[46] It called on the Air Force to: (1) "develop meaningful metrics to assess the performance of the TST processes, and develop procedures to measure TST process performance during combat operations," and (2) "study the relationship between TST doctrine and TST technology to determine the

---

[43] For example, an air strike in al-Shatra at 3:15 p.m. on April 4 killed six civilians and injured thirty-eight. Human Rights Watch interview with Dr. Salih Qadum, director, al-Shatra General Hospital, al-Shatra, May 27, 2003. This attack may have targeted `Ali Hassan al-Majid (known as "Chemical Ali"); al-Shatra is on the road to Basra, where the Coalition targeted al-Majid the next day. Four strikes in al-Rashidiyya, a town north of Baghdad, around 10:00 p.m. on April 6, killed forty-three civilians and injured twenty-four. Civilians reported that Saddam Hussein was rumored to be in the area and some said they saw an expensive Mercedes speeding through the streets before the bombs fell. Human Rights Watch interviews with `Ali Hirat `Abid, Hadi `Abid `Ali, `Abdullah Latif Hamid, `Abd al-Rahman `Abd al-Latif Ahmad, and Mahmud `Ali Hamada, al-Rashidiyya, October 16, 2003.

[44] This does not include attacks with armed Predator drones. These attacks are different from the others in that Predator allows visual confirmation of the target during strikes.

[45] "U.S. Planes Blitz Leaders' Compound," *South China Morning Post*, November 29, 2001.

[46] Leonard LaVella, "Operation Enduring Freedom Time Sensitive Targeting Process Study," Air Combat Command Analysis Division, Directorate of Requirements, August 25, 2003.

extent to which technology drives TST doctrine.[47] These criticisms and recommendations apply equally well to time-sensitive targeting in Iraq. The Air Force acknowledged that technology should not be the driving factor behind air strikes; just because a capability exists does not mean it should be used. It also recognized that the targeting process required an ability to measure effectiveness. In Iraq, the fascination with the ability to track targets via satellite phone and the inadequacies of the battle damage assessment process contributed to the failure of leadership targeting.

Flawed Targeting Methodology

In attacking leadership targets in Iraq, the United States used an unsound targeting methodology largely reliant on imprecise coordinates obtained from satellite phones. Leadership targeting was consistently based on unreliable intelligence. It is also likely that Iraqi leaders engaged in successful deception techniques. This combination of factors led directly to dozens of civilian casualties.

The United States identified and targeted some Iraqi leaders based on GPS coordinates derived from intercepts of Thuraya satellite phones.[48] Thuraya satellite phones are used throughout Iraq and the Middle East. They have an internal GPS chip that enabled American intelligence to track the phones. The phone coordinates were used as the locations for attacks on Iraqi leadership.

Targeting based on satellite phone-derived geo-coordinates turned a precision weapon into a potentially indiscriminate weapon. According to the manufacturer, Thuraya's GPS system is accurate only within a one-hundred-meter (328-foot) radius.[49] Thus the United States could not determine from where a call was originating to a degree of accuracy greater than one-hundred meters radius; a caller could have been anywhere within a 31,400-square-meter area. This begs the question, how did CENTCOM know

---

[47] Ibid.

[48] Michael Knights, "U.S.A. Learns Lessons in Time-Critical Targeting," *Jane's Intelligence Review*, July 1, 2003; Carl Cameron, "Intelligence Key to Strike on Leadership Target," FOX News, April 9, 2003, www.foxnews.com/story/0,2933,83611,00.html (retrieved October 21, 2003); "Tip about Hussein Leads to Fierce Baghdad Battle That Kills 1 Marine," Knight Ridder News Service, April 10, 2003; "Suspected Saddam Hideout Slammed by Fierce Bombing," Knight Ridder News Service, April 8, 2003; Brian Ross, Rhonda Schwartz, and Jill Rackmill, "Missed Opportunity? U.S. Attack May Have Ended Saddam Surrender Attempt," ABC News.com, April 21, 2003, http://abcnews.go.com/sections/wnt/World/iraq030421_missed_deal.html (retrieved October 20, 2003).

[49] Thuraya Satellite Telecommunications Company, "Extensive Roaming and Superior Connectivity," n.d., http://www.thuraya.com/products/services_marketing.htm (retrieved October 20, 2003). A user must be outside with an unobstructed view of the sky to receive a Thuraya signal.

where to direct the strike if the target area was so large? In essence, imprecise target coordinates were used to program precision-guided munitions.

Furthermore, it is not clear how CENTCOM connected a specific phone to a specific user; phones were being tracked, not individuals. It is plausible that CENTCOM developed a database of voices that could be computer matched to a phone user.

The Iraqis may have employed deception techniques to thwart the Americans. It was well known that the United States used intercepted Thuraya satellite phone calls in their search for members of al-Qaeda.[50] CENTCOM was so concerned about the possibility of the Iraqis turning the Thuraya intercept capability against U.S. forces that it ordered its troops to discontinue using Thuraya phones in early April 2003. It announced, "Recent intelligence reporting indicates Thuraya satellite phone services may have been compromised. For this reason, Thuraya phone use has been discontinued on the battlefields of Iraq. The phones now represent a security risk to units and personnel on the battlefield."[51] It is highly likely the Iraqi leaders assumed that the United States was attempting to track them through the Thuraya phones and therefore possible that they were spoofing American intelligence.

The United States undoubtedly attempted to use corroborating sources for satellite phone coordinates. Based on the results, however, accurate corroborating information must have been difficult if not impossible to come by and additional methods of tracking the Iraqi leadership just as unreliable as satellite phones.

Satellite imagery and signals intelligence (communications intercepts) apparently yielded little to no useful information in terms of targeting leadership. Detection of common indicators such as increased vehicular activity at particular locations seems not to have been meaningful. Human sources of information were likely the main means of corroborating the satellite phone information in tracking the Iraqi leadership. A human intelligence source was reportedly used to verify the Thuraya data acquired in the attack on Saddam Hussein in al-Mansur, described below.[52] But the source was proven wrong.

---

[50] Jason Burke, "Bin Laden Still Alive, Reveals Spy Satellite," *The Observer*, October 6, 2002; "Laden Is Alive and Regularly Meeting Omar: U.S. Report," *Times of India*, October 7, 2002; "FBI Tracking Muslims to Trace al-Qaeda Men," *The Pioneer*, October 7, 2002.

[51] U.S. CENTCOM, Headquarters, "Use of Thuraya Phones Discontinued," News Release 03-04-43, April 3, 2003.

[52] John Donnelly, "War in Iraq/Targeting the Leadership; After Airstrike, U.S. Seeks Clues on Fate of Hussein and Sons," *Boston Globe*, April 9, 2003, p. A21.

Human sources were also reportedly used to verify the attack on `Ali Hassan al-Majid in Basra, as well as the strike on al-Dura that opened the war.[53] Given the lack of success, it seems human intelligence was completely unreliable.

Without reliable intelligence to identify the location of the Iraqi leadership, it appears the United States fell back upon all it had, namely, inaccurate coordinates based on satellite phones, with no guarantee of the identity of the user. Leadership targets developed by inaccurate data should have never been attacked.

Given the dozens of civilian casualties caused by this profoundly flawed method of warfare, aerial attacks on leadership targets such as those witnessed in Iraq should be abandoned until the intelligence and targeting failures have been corrected. Like all attacks, leadership strikes should not be carried out without an adequate collateral damage estimate; strikes should not be based solely on satellite phone intercepts; and there should be no strikes in densely populated areas unless the intelligence is considered highly reliable. Consideration should also be given to possible alternative methods of attack posing less danger to civilians.[54]

Ineffective Battle Damage Assessment

The U.S. military's targeting methodology includes assessing the effectiveness of an attack after it is completed.[55] Battle damage assessment is considered necessary to evaluate the success or failure of an attack so that lessons learned can be applied and improvements made to future missions. BDA is carried out during a conflict as well as at the cessation of hostilities. Effective BDA can reduce the danger to civilians in war by allowing corrective actions to be taken.[56]

Although air strikes on Iraqi leadership repeatedly failed to hit their target and caused many civilian casualties, no decision was made during major combat operations to stop this practice. This was due at least in part to ineffective battle damage assessment. A

---

[53] Bradley Graham, "U.S. Moved Early for Air Supremacy."

[54] For example, attacks with armed Predator drones allow visual confirmation of the target during strikes.

[55] Major General Stanley McChrystal, "Coalition Targeting Procedures."

[56] An example of the potential effectiveness of BDA is the application of lessons learned in the NATO campaign in Yugoslavia during the war. Civilians were killed on the Djakovica-Decane Road when U.S. aircraft incorrectly identified civilian convoys as military in nature. The U.S. military and NATO learned what they were doing wrong and changed the rules of engagement. See Human Rights Watch, "Civilian Deaths in the NATO Air Campaign," p. 21.

senior CENTCOM official told Human Rights Watch that the BDA process is "broken." "The process cannot keep up with the pace of operations on the battlefield. The battlefield is moving and BDA can't keep up."[57]

Major General McChrystal of the Joint Chiefs of Staff stressed the degree to which the United States is concerned about collateral damage and effective battle damage assessment:

> [O]ne of the things I would highlight at the beginning, that we have proven already in this operation, as we said we would, every time we have a case where there is a real or even potential case of unintended civilian injury or death or collateral damage to structures, we've investigated it. And we go back and we look at the targeting; we account for every munition that, in fact, was suspended; we look for whether the aim points that we intended to hit were hit, to determine if, in fact, there was the result of our targeting unintended civilian damage—or casualties, or damage, and then we correct the errors as we go.[58]

With respect to the leadership attacks in Iraq it appears that effective BDA was not performed. The battle damage assessments should have led the United States to realize the leadership targeting was ineffective before a full fifty missions were flown. If attacks are repeatedly unsuccessful and result in significant civilian casualties, the entire target set should be reassessed. Leadership targeting should never have been allowed to reach such a high number of failed strikes that led to significant civilian deaths.

Case Studies of Attacks on Leadership Targets

Human Rights Watch's investigations in Iraq found that attacks on leadership likely resulted in the largest number of civilian deaths from the air war. The following case studies illustrate the impact on civilians of the flawed targeting methodology and intelligence used in leadership attacks.

---

[57] Human Rights Watch telephone interview with senior CENTCOM official #2.

[58] Major General Stanley McChrystal, "Coalition Targeting Procedures."

Al-Dura Farm, Baghdad

The war opened on March 20 with an attempted attack on Saddam Hussein. This strike was the beginning of a pattern that would be repeated many times. The U.S. military targeted a facility in the mistaken belief that the Iraqi leadership was there; instead of "decapitating" the regime, this strike resulted in fifteen civilian casualties because of faulty intelligence.

A human intelligence source provided the CIA with information on Saddam Hussein's alleged location at a farm in al-Dura, a district of southeastern Baghdad.[59] Two F-117A Nighthawk aircraft dropped four EGBU-27 2,000-pound penetrator bombs at 3:15 a.m. on a reported bunker at the farm. Moments later, the rest of the farm was hit with up to forty cruise missiles (Tomahawk Land Attack Missiles, or TLAMs) in an attempt to kill Saddam Hussein.[60] The U.S. military later acknowledged there was no bunker at the farm, and Saddam Hussein broadcast a television interview days later.[61] The attack resulted in one civilian killed and fourteen wounded, including nine women and a child.[62]

Al-Tuwaisi, Basra

U.S. aircraft bombed a building in al-Tuwaisi, a residential area in downtown Basra at approximately 5:20 a.m. on April 5, 2003, in an attempt to kill Lieutenant General `Ali Hassan al-Majid. Al-Majid, known as "Chemical Ali" because of his role in gassing the Kurds in the 1988 Anfal Campaign,[63] was in charge of southern Iraq during the recent war. Initial British reports indicated that al-Majid was killed in the attack. CENTCOM later reversed this claim and changed al-Majid's status back to "at large." Coalition forces ultimately captured al-Majid on August 21, 2003.[64]

---

[59] Barton Gellman and Dana Priest, "Surveillance Provided Unforeseen 'Target of Opportunity,'" *Washington Post*, March 20, 2003.

[60] Robert Burns, "Opening Round of War Targets Saddam; Iraq Fires at Troops," Associated Press, March 20, 2003.

[61] Bradley Graham, "U.S. Moved Early for Air Supremacy."

[62] Marian Wilkinson, "Decapitation Attempt Was Worth a Try, George," *Sydney Morning Herald*, March 22, 2003.

[63] See Human Rights Watch, *Genocide in Iraq: The Anfal Campaign Against the Kurds* (New York: Human Rights Watch, 1993).

[64] Bill Brink, "Former Iraqi Official Known as 'Chemical Ali' Is Captured," *New York Times*, August 21, 2003.

Basra: `Ali Hassan al-Majid ("Chemical Ali") Air Strike

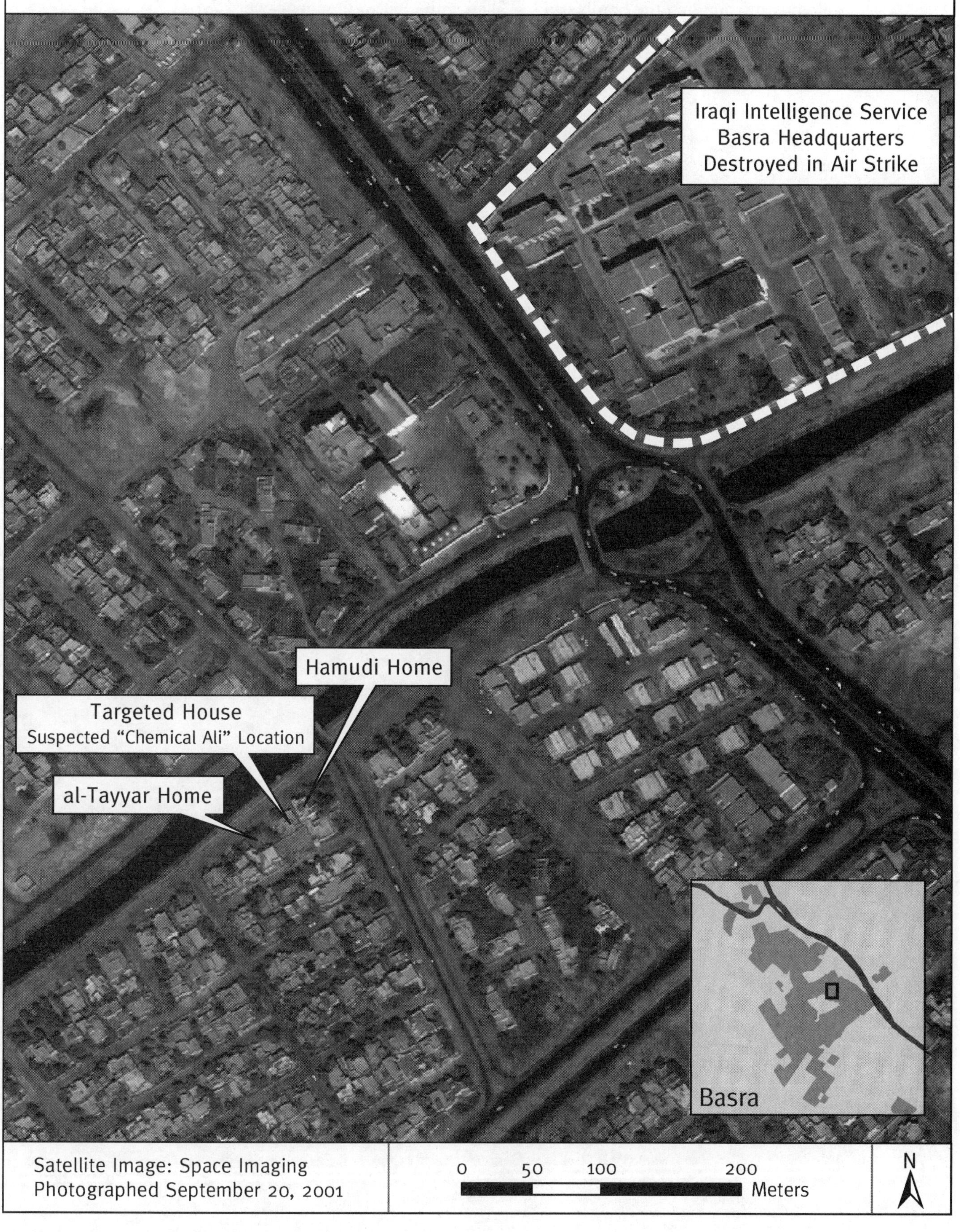

U.S. weapons hit the targeted building in the densely populated section of Basra, but the buildings surrounding the bomb strike—filled with civilian families—were also destroyed. Human Rights Watch investigators found that seventeen civilians were killed in this attack.[65]

The homes of the Hamudi and al-Tayyar families sat on either side of the building bombed by American forces. The homeowners gave Human Rights Watch conflicting reports of possible Iraqi government activity in the targeted building. `Abd al-Hussain Yunis al-Tayyar said there were members of the Iraqi Intelligence Service, or *Mukhabarat*, staying there, while `Abid Hassan Hamudi said it was vacant. Both denied any Iraqi leadership presence, as did all others interviewed. Al-Tayyar, Hamudi, and their families never saw al-Majid in the area.[66]

In the early morning hours of Saturday, April 5, al-Tayyar, a 50-year-old laborer, went to his garden to get water. Moments later an American bomb slammed into the targeted house next door, destroying his house as well. He picked himself up and immediately began to search the debris. He spent the rest of the day working to pull the dead bodies of his family from the rubble of his home, finally reaching his dead son at 4:00 p.m.[67]

The dead included:
1. As'ad `Abd al-Hussain al-Tayyar, 30, son
2. Qarar As'ad al-Tayyar, 12, grandson (son of As'ad)
3. Haidar As'ad al-Tayyar, 9, grandson (son of As'ad)
4. Saif As'ad al-Tayyar, 6, grandson (son of As'ad)
5. Intisar `Abd al-Hussain al-Tayyar, 30, daughter
6. Khawla `Ali al-Tayyar, 9, granddaughter (daughter of Intisar)
7. Hind `Ali al-Tayyar, 5, granddaughter (daughter of Intisar)

The Hamudi family home stood on the other side of the targeted house. `Abid Hassan Hamudi is a 70-year-old retired oil industry worker. His son, Dr. Akram Hamudi, is renowned in Basra as the senior surgeon at Basra Teaching Hospital. Dr. Hamudi spent

---

[65] Human Rights Watch interview with `Abd al-Hussain Yunis al-Tayyar, Basra, April 22, 2003; Human Rights Watch interview with `Abid Hassan Hamudi, Basra, April 22, 2003.

[66] Human Rights Watch interview with `Abd al-Hussain Yunis al-Tayyar; Human Rights Watch interview with `Abid Hassan Hamudi.

[67] Human Rights Watch interview with `Abd al-Hussain Yunis al-Tayyar.

the war in the hospital treating injured Iraqis. His family was staying in the Hamudi family home for safety, believing the Americans and British would never bomb civilians. In total, thirteen members of the extended family were living in a makeshift safe room made of reinforced concrete.[68]

`Abid Hamudi told Human Rights Watch that there were two bombs in the attack. The first bomb missed its target and slammed into the road a few hundred meters away, while the second hit the targeted home, also reducing his home to rubble. Hamudi was able to save three people, his daughter and her two sons, a five-year-old and six-year-old, all of whom were injured in the blast. The other ten people in his house perished.[69] "Why did this happen?" Hamudi asked a reporter. "Ten lives are gone. The house was completely destroyed. You came to save us, to protect us. That's what you said. It's now the contrary. Innocent people are killed."[70]

The dead included:

1. Dr. Khairiyya Shakir, 68, wife, gynecologist
2. Wisam `Abid Hassan, 38, son, computer engineer
3. Dr. Ihab `Abid Hassan, 34, son, gynecologist
4. Nura, 6 months, granddaughter (daughter of Dr. Ihab)
5. Zainab Akram, 19, granddaughter, pharmacist
6. Zain al-`Adidin Akram, 16, grandson
7. Mustafa Akram, 14, grandson
8. Hassan Iyad, 11, grandson
9. Zaina Akram, 12, granddaughter
10. `Amr Muhammad, 19 months, grandson

The size of the crater suggests that the weapon used in the April 5 attack was a 500-pound laser-guided bomb, the smallest PGM available. A second crater in the street a few hundred meters away, which is consistent with the crater found in the home, supports the assertion that the first bomb missed and was soon followed by another.[71]

---

[68] Human Rights Watch interview with `Abid Hassan Hamudi.

[69] Ibid.

[70] Keith B. Richburg, "In Basra, Growing Resentment, Little Aid; Casualties Stoke Hostility Over British Presence," *Washington Post*, April 9, 2003, p. A23.

[71] The precision-guided munition may have missed its target due to mechanical, electrical, or human error.

The collateral damage estimate done on the target appears to have allowed for a high level of civilian damage. This attack may have been approved due to the perceived military value of al-Majid. Had smaller weapons been used, however, many civilian lives may have been spared. A senior CENTCOM official told Human Rights Watch that the U.S. military needs smaller munitions with lower yields that will reduce collateral damage.[72]

Al-Karrada, Baghdad

On April 8, Sa`dun Hassan Salih lifted his nephew's two-month-old daughter, Dina, from the grass in front of the smoking hole that had been her home. She was alive, both arms and legs broken, but she was orphaned. Her family had been staying in Salih's home in the affluent al-Karrada neighborhood of Baghdad, secure in the belief that such a densely populated area of the city would not be targeted. But they would often return to their home, one mile (1.6 kilometers) away, to get some clothes or other things they needed. "That night they went home to get some belongings," said Salih. "We all felt safer together as a family. If we were going to die, we would die together. But no one would bomb a home. My nephew was the last to leave the house, around 9:00 p.m., in his car. That is the last time I ever saw him."[73]

Minutes later, two bombs, seconds apart, destroyed Zaid Ratha Jabir's home and those inside. Incredibly, Dina survived. She was blown out of the home by the blast and now lives with Salih and his wife, `Imad Hassun Salih. At first they were filled with grief, but now they are angry. "The Americans said no civilians were targeted," said `Imad. "I don't understand how this could happen."[74]

According to Salih, there were no obvious military targets in the area. He speculated that a bitter family rival lied to the Americans. He said, "Perhaps someone wanted to kill them because of jealousy and told them [the Americans] Saddam or one of his men were there. But my family had no dealings with the regime. We hate Saddam."[75]

---

[72] Human Rights Watch telephone interview with senior CENTCOM official #2.

[73] Human Rights Watch interview with Sa'dun Hassan Salih, Baghdad, May 18, 2003.

[74] Human Rights Watch interview with `Imad Hassan Salih, Baghdad, May 18, 2003.

[75] Human Rights Watch interview with Sa'dun Hassan Salih.

Baghdad: Decapitation Strike in al-Karrada

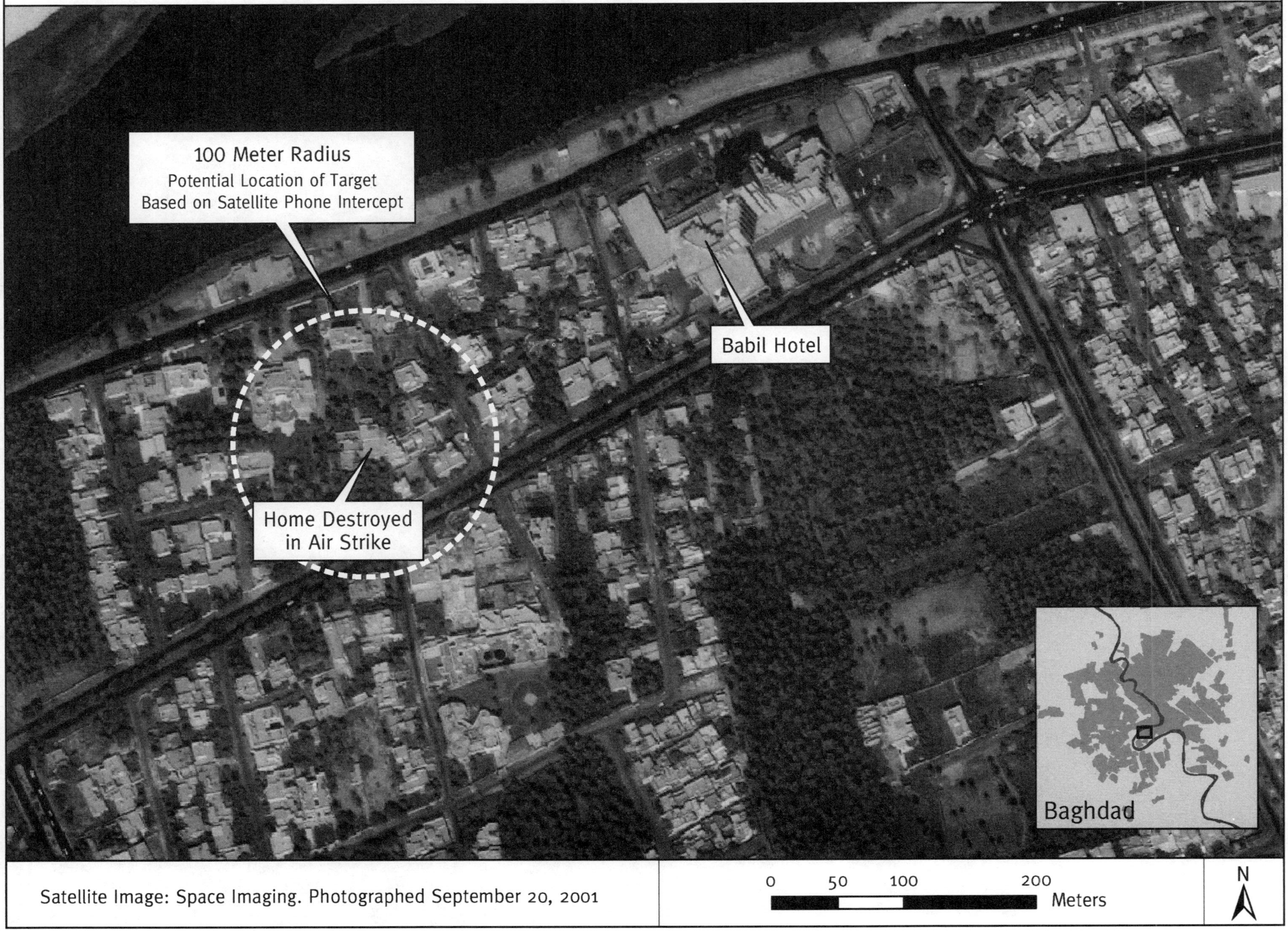

Satellite Image: Space Imaging. Photographed September 20, 2001

A Department of Defense official told Human Rights Watch that Saddam Hussein's half-brother Watban was the intended target of this air strike, and that he was identified through poor communications security.[76] This was likely a Thuraya intercept. Watban was eventually captured near the Syrian-Iraqi border near the end of the war almost a week later.

"It was a mistake. I don't know why the house was hit. There was no intelligence, no army nearby, no weapons. Why did Americans tell the world they hit only places of the army? Why did they hit civilian homes?" asked a distraught Salih.[77]

The dead included:
1. Zaid Ratha Jabir, 36, engineer
2. Rana, 25, his wife
3. Mina, 2, his daughter
4. Mulkiyya, 87, his aunt
5. Zahida, 34, Zaid's sister
6. `Adhra, 32, Zaid's sister

The attack also destroyed the house next door, which belonged to the brother of Sa`ad `Abd al-Rasul `Ali. `Ali said he and his family had left Iraq during the war so no one from this house was injured. He had heard rumors that Saddam Hussein had been in the neighborhood around the time of the strike but described them as "only propaganda."[78]

---

[76] Human Rights Watch interview with Department of Defense official.

[77] Human Rights Watch interview with Sa'dun Hassan Salih.

[78] Human Rights Watch interview with Sa`ad `Abd al-Rasul `Ali, Baghdad, May 17, 2003.

U.S. bombs destroyed this home in al-Karrada during an attempted leadership strike on Saddam Hussein's half-brother Watban. Of the seven family members inside, only four-month-old Dina Jabir survived. The explosion threw her out of the house and she was found the next day in a neighbor's garden. © 2003 Bonnie Docherty / Human Rights Watch

Four-month-old Dina Jabir is held by her uncle Sa`dun Hassan Salih. Dina's family died during an air strike in al-Karrada neighborhood of Baghdad intended for Saddam Hussein's half-brother Watban, who was captured a week later. Dina was blown out of the home by a U.S. precision bomb and found in a field the next morning suffering from broken bones and orphaned, but alive. © 2003 Marc Garlasco / Human Rights Watch

Baghdad: al-Mansur District Decapitation Strike

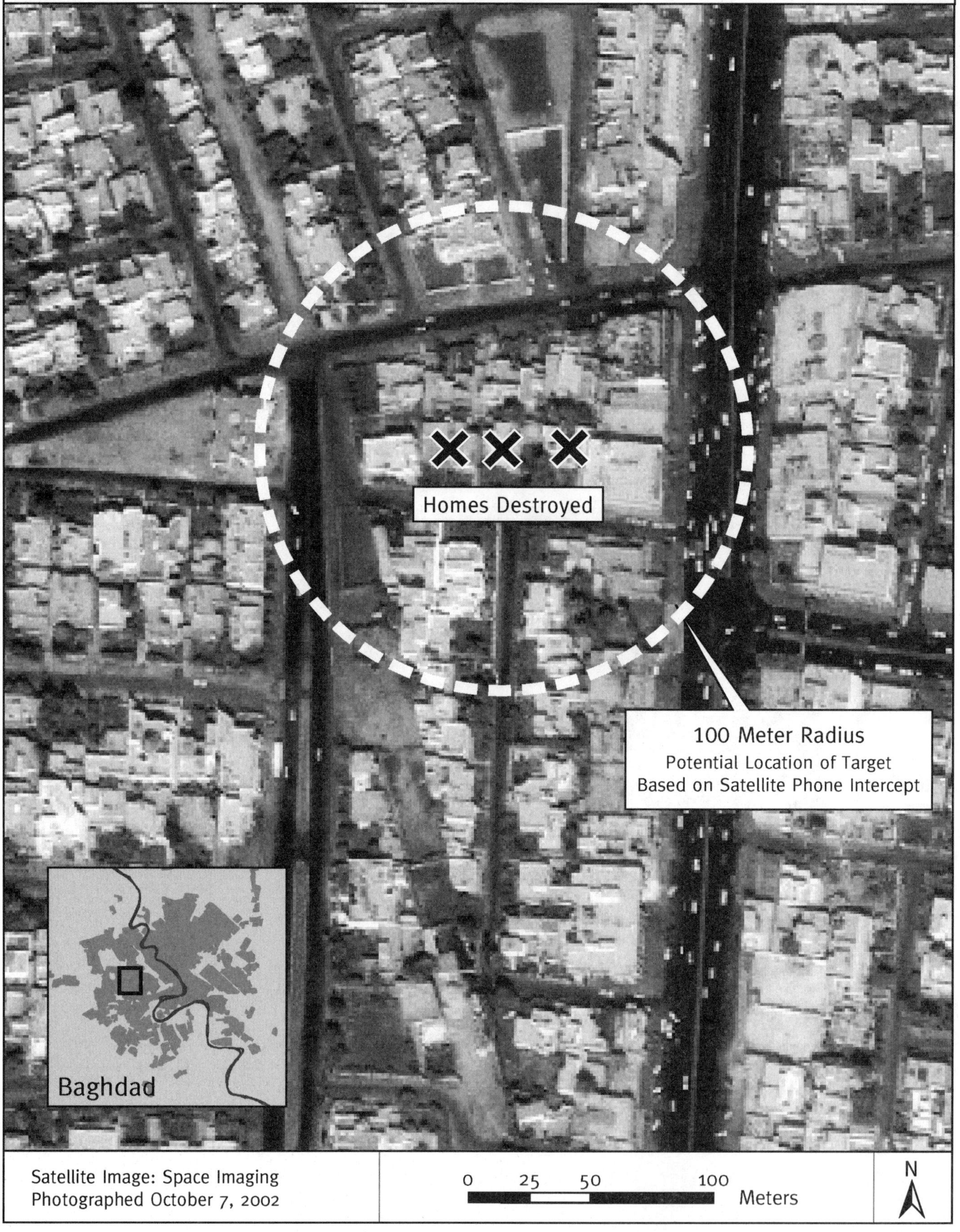

Al-Mansur, Baghdad

On April 7, a U.S. Air Force B-1B Lancer aircraft dropped four 2,000-pound satellite-guided Joint Direct Attack Munitions (JDAMs) on a house in al-Mansur district of Baghdad.[79] The attack killed an estimated eighteen civilians.

U.S. intelligence indicated that Saddam Hussein and perhaps one or both of his sons were meeting in al-Mansur.[80] The information was reportedly based on a communications intercept of a Thuraya satellite phone. Forty-five minutes later the area was rubble.[81]

This was the most publicized of the leadership strikes. The U.S. military lauded the short turn-around time "from sensor to shooter," the time it takes from development of information to when the strike is executed. "From start to finish, it took 45 minutes from the word that Saddam Hussein and other leaders may have entered the building until the bombs hit the structure," said Major General McChrystal.[82]

A Department of Defense official told Human Rights Watch, however, that an inadequate collateral damage estimate was done due to the time constraints.[83] Forty-five minutes, including the approximately twelve minutes it took the B-1B to fly the mission, was little time to take the raw data of the time and location of the meeting, interpret it, prepare and target the mission, and pass it up the chain in CENTCOM for the decision to make the strike.[84]

The effects of the strike were stark, a huge crater surrounded by damaged homes. Interviews with residents of the area and press reports indicated approximately eighteen civilians died in the strike. Ahmad al-Sibi, whose house was behind the bomb crater, stated that his home became "like a wave of water" when the bombs struck. He saw

---

[79] David Blair, "Smart Bombs Aimed at Saddam Killed Families," *Daily Telegraph*, April 21, 2003, p. 11.

[80] John Donnelly, "War in Iraq/Targeting the Leadership; After Airstrike, U.S. Seeks Clues on Fate of Hussein and Sons."

[81] "Saddam May Be Dead," Knight Ridder Newspapers, April 8, 2003.

[82] John Donnelly, "War in Iraq/Targeting the Leadership; After Airstrike, U.S. Seeks Clues on Fate of Hussein and Sons."

[83] Human Rights Watch interview with Department of Defense official.

[84] Mark Thompson and Timothy J. Burger, "How to Attack a Dictator, Part II," *Time*, April 21, 2003.

three houses fall. He said there was no evidence that Saddam Hussein or any members of the Iraqi government had been there.[85]

Pentagon officials admitted that they did not know precisely who was at the targeted location. "What we have for battle damage assessment right now is essentially a hole in the ground, a site of destruction where we wanted it to be, where we believe high-value targets were. We do not have a hard and fast assessment of what individual or individuals were on site," said Major General McChrystal.[86]

One intelligence official was quoted as saying that since the U.S. military was unsure if Saddam was killed in the strike on al-Dura farm, "just in case he didn't die before, let's have him die again."[87] In May, Vice President Dick Cheney said about the strike, "I think we did get Saddam Hussein. He was seen being dug out of the rubble and wasn't able to breathe."[88] The U.S. government, however, has subsequently said it appears that Saddam Hussein was not killed in the strike; multiple radio announcements attributed to him since the bombing have been judged as probably authentic.[89]

This strike shows that targeting based on satellite phones is seriously flawed. Even if the targeted individual is actually determined to be on the phone, the person could be far from the impact point. The GBU-31s dropped on al-Mansur have a published accuracy of thirteen meters (forty-three feet) circular error probable (CEP), while the phone coordinates are accurate only to a one-hundred-meter (328-foot) radius.[90] The weapon was inherently more accurate than the information used to determine its target, which led to substantial civilian casualties with no military advantages. U.S. military leaders defended these attacks even after revelations that the strikes resulted in civilian deaths instead of the deaths of the intended targets. One said that the strikes "demonstrated U.S. resolve and capabilities."[91]

---

[85] Human Rights Watch interview with Ahmad al-Sibi, Baghdad, May 22, 2003.

[86] Rowan Scarborough, "Saddam Seen at Site," *Washington Times*, April 9, 2003.

[87] Mark Thompson and Timothy J. Burger, "How to Attack a Dictator, Part II."

[88] David Rohde, "Bomb Crater Probed in Search for Saddam," *New York Times*, June 6, 2003, p. A1.

[89] "Bremer Says Saddam Alive, Not Behind Attacks," Associated Press, July 21, 2003; Guy Taylor, "CIA Says Al Jazeera Audiotape 'Most Likely' Saddam," *Washington Times*, July 8, 2003; "CIA Reported to Believe Saddam is Alive," United Press International, June 3, 2003.

[90] CEP is "the radius of a circle within which half of a missile's projectiles are expected to fall." U.S. Department of Defense, "Dictionary of Military Terms," June 5, 2003, http://www.dtic.mil/doctrine/jel/doddict (retrieved October 21, 2003).

[91] Bradley Graham, "U.S. Moved Early for Air Supremacy."

This crater in al-Mansur district of Baghdad is all that remains of three homes destroyed in a U.S. air strike targeting Saddam Hussein on April 7, 2003. Eighteen civilians were killed in the strike. © 2003 Marc Garlasco / Human Rights Watch

Conclusion and Recommendations

Under international humanitarian law, the targeting of military leadership is permissible, even if it results in civilian casualties, so long as the anticipated concrete and direct military advantage outweighs the civilian cost. Aerial strikes targeting the leadership of a party to the conflict ("decapitation strikes" in U.S. military parlance) are governed by the same rules of IHL that apply to other military actions: the individual attacked must be a military target[92] and the attack must not be indiscriminate, i.e., it must distinguish between civilians and combatants, and it must not cause harm to the civilian population or civilian objects which could be "excessive in relation to the concrete and direct military advantage anticipated" from the attack.[93] Human Rights Watch did not assess the military advantage of eliminating specific Iraqi military leaders, but the United States is required to carry out this balancing act prior to launching decapitation strikes.

If they respect these criteria, attacks on enemy leaders who take a direct part in hostilities are not prohibited and are different from assassinations committed outside the context of an armed conflict, which are extrajudicial executions prohibited by international human rights law.[94] Aerial strikes on leadership targets, however, still require a particularly high level of scrutiny.

The U.S. practice of decapitation strikes gives rise to a number of concerns. In some cases, the location of the intended target and the imprecision of the coordinates used to direct the attack may have resulted in indiscriminate attacks. More generally, the continued resort to decapitation strikes despite their complete lack of success and the significant civilian losses they caused can be seen as a failure to take "all feasible precautions" in choice of means and methods of warfare in order to minimize civilian losses as required by international humanitarian law.[95]

---

[92] Protocol I, arts. 48, 52(2).

[93] Ibid., arts. 51(5)(b), 57(2).

[94] Since 1976, successive U.S. presidents, including President George W. Bush, have endorsed an executive order (Executive Order 12333) banning political assassinations. This order followed revelations of earlier U.S. assassinations and assassination attempts of various world leaders. Consonant with the rules outlined above, this order does not prohibit targeting enemy combatants and their commanders in an armed conflict, and it does not prohibit the use of lethal force by law enforcement agents when necessary to avoid imminent death or serious injury. But it rightfully prohibits summary execution in any circumstance and the targeted killing of people (other than combatants in armed conflict) in lieu of invoking available criminal justice remedies. See Executive Order 12333 of December 4, 1981, 3 C.F.R. 200 (1981 comp.).

[95] Protocol I, art. 57(2)(a).

The U.S. armed forces should perform a thorough investigation of the battle damage assessment process, determine how it can be improved to mitigate civilian casualties, and implement appropriate changes.

Human Rights Watch recommends that if the United States bombs populated areas, it should:

- Complete a collateral damage estimate in advance and balance this against the expected direct and concrete military advantage of the attack.
- Use the smallest effective precision munitions to limit civilian harm.
- Carry out a bomb damage assessment as soon as possible after the attack and apply immediate lessons learned.

The United States has committed itself to all these steps, but it needs to implement them more consistently.

Human Rights Watch also recommends that the United States abandon aerial attacks on leadership targets until the targeting and intelligence failures have been corrected. In particular,

- Strikes should not be based solely on satellite phone intercepts.
- There should be no strikes in densely populated areas unless the intelligence is considered highly reliable.

Preplanned Targets

Strategic targeting consists of preplanned missions against fixed facilities. In Iraq, Coalition forces attacked most of these in the first few days of the war with cruise missiles and other precision-guided munitions. This targeting was characterized by strikes designed to destroy, degrade, or deny the ability to command and control Iraqi forces and/or employ weapons of mass destruction. Preplanned targets included leadership, government, security, and military facilities, and certain dual-use infrastructure elements (such as electrical power, media, and telecommunications facilities).[96]

---

[96] Human Rights Watch telephone interview with senior CENTCOM official #2.

Off Target

Attacks on these facilities generally did not result in civilian casualties or extensive damage to civilian property for a number of reasons. U.S. strategy avoided power plants, public water facilities, refineries, bridges, and other civilian structures. Most of the facilities that were hit were in areas to which the civilian population did not have access. Thorough collateral damage estimates were done for each of the preplanned targets. Finally, these attacks were carried out exclusively with precision-guided munitions.

Human Rights Watch's investigations found, however, that air strikes on civilian power facilities in al-Nasiriyya caused serious civilian suffering and that the legality of the attacks on media installations is questionable.

Dual-Use Targets

Dual-use facilities are those that can have both a military and civilian application. In Iraq, the United States and United Kingdom considered electrical power, media, and telecommunications installations dual use and attacked examples of each. In some instances, however, it was not clear to Human Rights Watch why Coalition forces characterized certain installations in that way. A dual-use object may be a legitimate military target because it makes an "effective contribution to military action" and its destruction offers "a definite military advantage."[97] Yet the harm to the civilian population in its destruction may be disproportionate to the expected "concrete and direct military advantage," rendering an attack impermissible.[98] In assessing potential targets, military planners must carefully balance the concrete and direct military advantage of destroying these facilities against the expected death and injury to civilians and damage to civilian objects.[99]

Electrical Power Facilities

The United States targeted electrical power distribution facilities, but not generation facilities, throughout Iraq, according to a senior CENTCOM official. He told Human Rights Watch that instead of using explosive ordnance, the majority of the attacks were carried out with carbon fiber bombs designed to incapacitate temporarily rather than to destroy.[100] Nevertheless, some of the attacks on electrical power distribution facilities in

---

[97] Protocol I, art. 52(2).

[98] Ibid., art. 51(5)(b).

[99] Ibid.

[100] Human Rights Watch telephone interview with senior CENTCOM official #2.

Iraq are likely to have a serious and long-term detrimental impact on the civilian population.

Electrical power was out for thirty days after U.S. strikes on two transformer facilities in al-Nasiriyya.[101] Al-Nasiriyya 400 kV Electrical Power Transformer Station was attacked on March 22 at 6:00 a.m. using three U.S. Navy Tomahawk cruise missiles outfitted with variants of the BLU-114/B graphite bombs.[102] These dispense submunitions with spools of carbon fiber filaments that short-circuit transformers and other high voltage equipment upon contact.

The United States attacked al-Nasiriyya 400 kV Electrical Power Transformer Station on March 22, 2003, with a carbon fiber bomb designed to disable power. The city lost power for thirty days. © 2003 Reuben E. Brigety, II / Human Rights Watch

---

[101] Human Rights Watch interview with `Ali Bashi Jabbar, chief of operations of electricity, al-Nasiriyya, May 9, 2003.

[102] BLU stands for "bomb live unit" and is often used to designate the submunitions in cluster munitions.

The transformer station is the critical link between al-Nasiriyya Electrical Power Production Plant and the city of al-Nasiriyya.[103] When the transformer station went off-line it removed the southern link to all power in the city, which was then totally reliant on the North Electrical Station 132. Although the carbon fiber is supposed to incapacitate temporarily, three transformers were completely destroyed by a fire from a short circuit caused by the carbon fiber. The station's wires seemed to have been melted by the intense fire. Human Rights Watch was told that the transformers would have to be replaced and the entire facility rewired.

On March 23 at 10:00 a.m., the United States attacked North Electrical Station 132. Hassan Dawud, an engineer at the station when it was attacked, said a U.S. aircraft strafed the facility, destroying three transformers, gas pipes, and the air conditioning, which brought the entire facility down as components that were not damaged by the attack overheated.[104] Damage to the transformers and air conditioning were clearly visible, including large holes in the walls consistent with aircraft cannon fire. Further north in Rafi on Highway 7, Human Rights Watch found a transformer station with significant damage from air strikes, including at least one destroyed transformer.

From its investigations, it is unclear to Human Rights Watch what effective contribution to Iraqi military action these facilities were making and why attacking them offered a definite military advantage to the United States, and in particular how they supported the ground operations in al-Nasiriyya. Two senior CENTCOM officials declined to comment on these attacks.[105] Human Rights Watch does not understand the military necessity and rationale for these attacks and calls on the United States to explain them fully.

The attacks caused significant and long-term damage, and the civilian cost was high. Dr. `Ali `Abd al-Sayyid, director of al-Nasiriyya General Hospital, told Human Rights Watch that the loss of power was a huge impediment to the proper treatment of war wounded. No one died as a direct result of the power loss, but the hospital's generators were taxed to their limit and it had to do away with some non-critical services to ensure the

---

[103] Human Rights Watch interview with Hamid Kadhim, engineer in charge, al-Nasiriyya Electrical Power Plant, al-Nasiriyya, May 9, 2003; Human Rights Watch interview with `Ali Dakhil, security manager, al-Nasiriyya Electrical Power Plant, al-Nasiriyya, May 9, 2003. Dakhil was at the station the morning of the attack.

[104] Human Rights Watch interview with Hassan Dawud, engineer, North Electrical Station 132, al-Nasiriyya, May 9, 2003.

[105] Human Rights Watch telephone interview with senior CENTCOM official #1; Human Rights Watch telephone interview with senior CENTCOM official #2.

wounded were given basic treatment. He also stated that the loss of power created a water crisis in the city.[106]

Human Rights Watch researchers saw many areas in al-Nasiriyya where people had dug up water and sewage pipes outside their homes in a vain attempt to get drinking water. Even when successful, the water was often contaminated because the power outage prevented water purification. This led to what Dr. `Abd al-Sayyid termed "water-born diarrheal infections."[107]

Human Rights Watch believes that extreme caution should be used in the targeting of electrical power facilities because of the potential profound and long-term impact on civilian populations. The loss of electrical power in the first Gulf War, for example, crippled basic civilian services, including hospital-based medical care, and shut down water distribution, water purification, and sewage treatment plants. This led to death and suffering, especially among the most vulnerable members of the population.[108]

In particular, Human Rights Watch believes that civilian electrical generation (production) facilities should not be attacked because replacement is costly and time-consuming, thereby causing prolonged human suffering. As seen in Yugoslavia, attacks on electrical distribution facilities can have a lesser impact. If distribution facilities are attacked, it should be done in such as way as to cause only temporarily incapacitation.

Al-Nasiriyya case is positive in some respects. Power distribution—not power generation—was targeted. Although it took a month for power to be fully restored, it would have taken much longer to rebuild an entire power production plant. The use of carbon fiber weapons may have prevented civilian casualties at the facility and allowed for quicker repair.

---

[106] Human Rights Watch interview with Dr. `Ali `Abd al-Sayyid, director, al-Nasiriyya General Hospital, al-Nasiriyya, May 7, 2003.

[107] Ibid.

[108] Human Rights Watch, *Needless Deaths in the Gulf War: Civilian Casualties During the Air Campaign and Violations of the Laws of War* (New York: Human Rights Watch, 1991), pp. 180-85.

The United States dropped these carbon fiber filaments in an attack on electrical power in al-Nasiriyya. These filaments are designed to disable power, but in this case they caused a fire that destroyed the transformer station and plunged the city into darkness for thirty days. © 2003 Marc Garlasco / Human Rights Watch

Media Installations

Human Rights Watch researchers visited three media facilities in Baghdad hit by U.S. air strikes: the Ministry of Information, the Baghdad Television Studio and Broadcast Facility, and the Abu Ghraib Television Antennae Broadcast Facility. While special care seems to have been taken to avoid civilian casualties when attacking the Ministry of Information, the latter two facilities were completely destroyed. There were no recorded civilian casualties as a result of any of these attacks.

The March 28 attack on the Ministry of Information was carried out with the CBU-107 Passive Attack Weapon, marking its first use in combat.[109] The CBU-107, nicknamed the "rods from God" by the U.S. military, is a new non-explosive cluster bomb that contains 3,700 inert metal rods designed to destroy "soft" targets, i.e., those without armor. In this case, two CBU-107s were used to remove antennae on the roof of the

---

[109] Human Rights Watch telephone interview with senior CENTCOM official #2. CBU stands for "cluster bomb unit."

Baghdad: Attacks on State Media

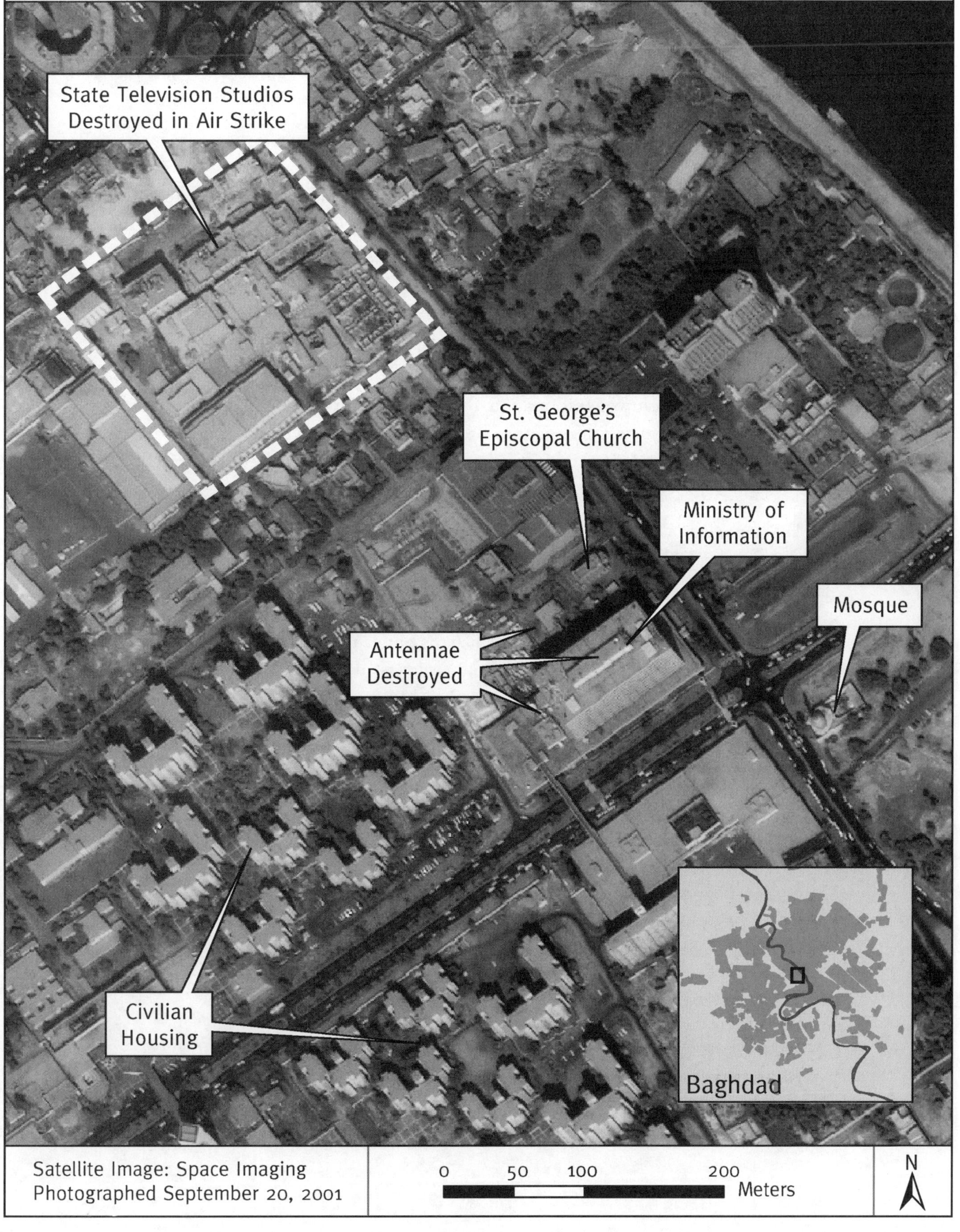

building without destroying the facility. The custodian of Saint George's Episcopal Church, next door to the ministry, told Human Rights Watch of seeing a series of bombs in the sky over the ministry.[110] Visible observation of the facility confirmed that there was little to no structural damage done by the air strike, though the antennae were destroyed. The church adjacent to and a mosque across the street from the ministry suffered minimal damage, primarily broken windows, in the attack.

Prior to this attack the United States had used a Predator drone armed with a Hellfire missile to destroy a single uplink antenna at this facility. The use of the armed Predator allowed CENTCOM to confirm visually there were no civilians in the area during the attack. The Predator also had a smaller warhead than the majority of bombs dropped during the war, thereby reducing damage to the area and the potential for civilian casualties.

In contrast to the Ministry of Information, the Television Studio and Broadcast Facility and the Abu Ghraib Television Antennae Broadcast Facility were completely destroyed. The former is in a Baghdad business district, while the latter is in an isolated area.

The U.S. targeting of the television broadcast capabilities of Iraq appears to have been aimed at denying Saddam Hussein and his government the ability to broadcast official statements on television. The United States attempted to end Iraqi government broadcasts by destroying television facilities but failed to do so until April 8, the day before Baghdad fell. The Iraqi authorities, like the Serbian authorities before them, maintained television broadcasts by using mobile assets and redundant broadcast capabilities.[111]

A senior CENTCOM official told Human Rights Watch,

> The personality of the regime used the tool of the media. . . . It was clear we needed to eliminate the regime's ability to put out disinformation. . . . Most important was the Iraqi TV's military value. We have felt pretty comfortable that it was one of the means Iraqi intelligence used to signal its elements outside the country. . . . There was a potential for terrorist activity. . . . Did it happen? No. We were concerned it would happen,

---

[110] Human Rights Watch interview with custodian, St. George's Episcopal Church, Baghdad, May 17, 2003.

[111] In the 1999 Kosovo conflict, Radio Television Serbia, a central Belgrade broadcast facility, was targeted, and many civilians were killed. See Human Rights Watch, "Civilian Deaths in the NATO Air Campaign," p. 26.

felt the potential for a catastrophic event outweighed the potential ill
will. But the Iraqis never used TV to direct the military. There were
songs we knew of they could use and had in the past that would tell
forces where to go and to take certain actions. This is why we took out
TV.[112]

There is no evidence that Iraqi media was being used to provide direct assistance to the
Iraqi armed forces. If the media is used to incite violence, as in Rwanda, or to direct
troops, it may become a legitimate target. The media facilities in Iraq, however, did not
appear to be making an effective contribution to military action. As a consequence,
Human Rights Watch believes that while stopping broadcasts intended to give
encouragement to the general population may have served to demoralize the Iraqi
population and undermine the government's political support, neither purpose offered
the definite military advantage required by law to make media facilities legitimate military
targets.

Civilian Telecommunications Facilities

U.S. attacks largely destroyed the telecommunications infrastructure in Iraq. The main
telecommunication gateway switches Sinek and Ma'mun were both destroyed by GBU-
37/B 5,000-pound guided bombs.[113] Their destruction removed all long-distance calling
capability from Iraq to the outside world. There were no reported civilian casualties in
the attacks on these facilities, probably because of the timing and weapon choice. The
attacks all took place at night when the chance of civilians being present was lessened.
The bombs used were penetrators, which are designed to bury deep inside a target
before exploding, therefore imploding the building and minimizing damage to the
surrounding area.

Other telecommunications exchanges in Baghdad were also destroyed, though smaller
munitions were used. In many of the strikes on telecommunications facilities, the
United States targeted and destroyed cable vaults leaving the facilities relatively
undamaged, which should facilitate their reconstruction. Post-war looting, however,
rendered these precautions irrelevant because thieves picked most of the facilities clean.

---

[112] Human Rights Watch telephone interview with senior CENTCOM official #2.

[113] "Bunker-Buster Dropped on Baghdad," CNN.com, March 28, 2003,
http://www.cnn.com/2003/WORLD/meast/03/27/sprj.irq.war.int.main/index.html (retrieved October 20, 2003).

According to a senior CENTCOM official:

> We waited very long to hit civil telecoms. Military comms were
> automatic. But Iraq had spent a lot of money and time on contracts
> with China, France, and Yugoslavia setting up a modern fiber optic and
> coaxial cable telecoms network to support the military comms. We took
> a shoot-listen-shoot approach. We knew the risk was giving the Iraqi
> propaganda an opportunity to stay on the network. The principal
> objective early on was to sever command and control for fielded forces.
> The Iraqi military had a very central command and control process. If
> we could eliminate high-level commands, the regional and local
> commands became autonomous and many were less likely to die for
> their country if they didn't feel directly supervised and had no
> commands from the leadership. . . . This reduced the likelihood of street
> fighting in Baghdad.[114]

Government Facilities

Preplanned targets primarily included leadership buildings, government buildings, and
security buildings. These attacks, carried out by the United States solely with precision-
guided munitions, led to few known civilian casualties. In addition to the accuracy of
such weapons, thorough collateral damage estimates helped minimize the civilian toll.
Human Rights Watch researchers also noted instances where weapon choice and fuzing
contributed to the low casualty rate from bombing. Moreover, civilian casualties were
limited by Iraq's policy of locating the majority of these facilities away from the
population. Even where these facilities were in populated areas, they were often
separated by security perimeters and walls.

The methodology used in U.S. attacks on government buildings, and the success in
avoiding civilian casualties, stands in stark contrast to other U.S. attacks, particularly
those targeting leadership and those involving cluster bombs. The United States took
extensive precautions to avoid civilian casualties and other civilian harm when planning
and executing attacks on strategic targets such as government facilities. Because of these
precautions, there were few civilian casualties even in densely populated areas. Having
demonstrated its ability to do so, the United States should apply the same level of care
and consideration in targeting and executing other air attacks as in the cases below.

---

[114] Human Rights Watch telephone interview with senior CENTCOM official #2.

The Republican Palace Complex and Other Government Buildings

Throughout Baghdad, Human Rights Watch researchers found bombed government, intelligence, and security facilities. The use of precision-guided weapons combined with the fact that most of these facilities were designed by the government to limit access by the civilian population, however, minimized civilian casualties. The Republican Palace complex in downtown Baghdad contained the Republican Palace, the Revolutionary Command Council buildings, the Presidential Secretariat, Saddam's Bunker, the Ministry of Planning, and offices and living quarters for Saddam Hussein's guards. Tomahawk cruise missiles and JDAMs hit the entire area, except for the Republican Palace, which was not bombed during the war and currently serves as the headquarters for the Coalition Provisional Authority. The palace complex had always been completely off limits to all civilians, and Baghdadis told Human Rights Watch researchers that the area had been deserted for days as government officials expected the attacks.

Another good example is the Iraqi Intelligence Service Headquarters, a sprawling complex with many buildings in the center of a populated area in al-Mansur district of Baghdad. Due to the high walls and location of buildings in the center of the compound and the accuracy of the precision-guided weapons, there were apparently no civilian casualties from the air strikes.

Attacks on buildings without such protection had similar results. Human Rights Watch was told the headquarters of the Baghdad Emergency Forces was struck by a GBU-37 5,000-pound penetrator bomb.[115] This multistory building is a few hundred yards from an apartment complex, but the apartment windows were still intact. It appears that the penetrating nature of the weapon contained the blast and fragmentation damage.

Baghdad International Fairgrounds

U.S. forces attacked the Baghdad International Fairgrounds, which had been occupied by the Iraqi Intelligence Service. The fairgrounds consisted of dozens of buildings used for trade shows and business conventions. Across the street from the fairgrounds is the Baghdad Red Crescent Maternity Hospital; Human Rights Watch spoke to the director, Dr. Rasmi al-Rikabi. He said that the *Mukhabarat* had left their headquarters complex in al-Mansur district and had occupied the Fairgrounds and his hospital. The hospital had been evacuated two weeks earlier, but a skeleton staff remained and watched as the *Mukhabarat* freely operated from the hospital. Dr. al-Rikabi said that the *Mukhabarat*

---

[115] Human Rights Watch interview with U.S. Air Force officer, Baghdad, May 2003.

Baghdad: Air Strike on Fairgrounds Adjacent to Red Crescent Maternity Hospital

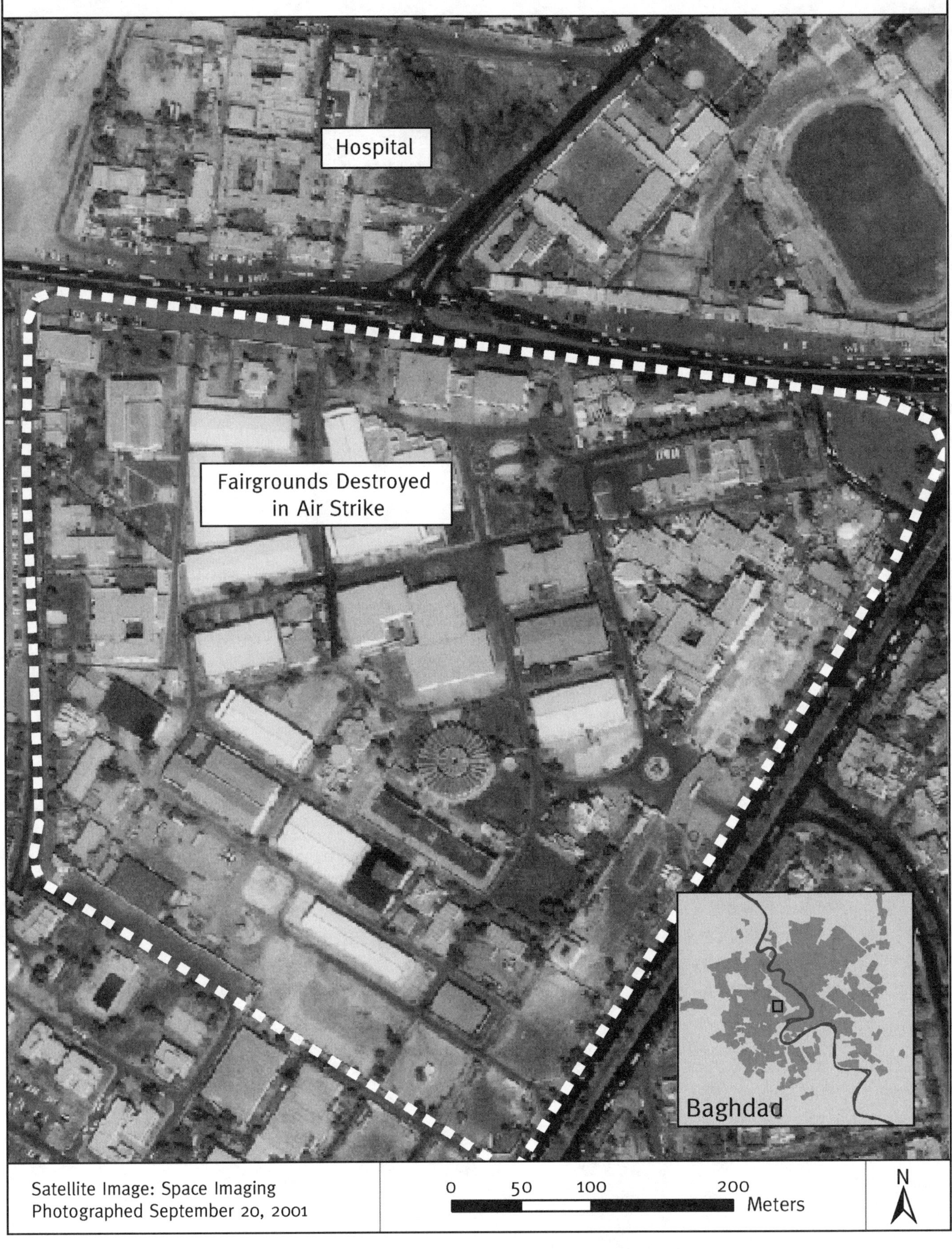

threatened to kill him if he questioned their presence so he remained silent.[116]

At 9:00 a.m. on April 2, nine 2,000-pound precision-guided bombs struck the International Fairgrounds, blowing the glass out of the hospital and partially collapsing a secondary roof. One person in the street was killed and twenty-five or so suffered minor injuries, mostly from glass. The *Mukhabarat* evacuated the area and Dr. al-Rikabi treated the wounded.[117]

It appears the United States took precautions to minimize civilian casualties. Though 18,000 pounds of bombs were dropped some one hundred yards (ninety meters) away from the hospital, the angle of the attack seems to have limited the blast and fragmentation damage and directed it away from the hospital. There also appears to be some evidence of delayed fuzing, which caused the buildings to implode and thus contained damage.

Directorate of General Security Facilities

The Directorate of General Security (DGS), the Iraqi security organization responsible for monitoring political dissent, was a fixture throughout Iraq. During the war, DGS was responsible for coordinating local militias. There were DGS offices in most Iraqi cities, and all had prison cells and basement holding cells where Iraqi dissidents were tortured and killed. DGS facilities served as stark reminders to the population of their expected loyalty to Saddam Hussein, and as such were placed close to civilian facilities. In al-Nasiriyya, for example, the DGS headquarters building stood across the street from the General Hospital. In Basra it was across from the courthouse and other civil establishments. The presence of above ground prisons complicated the targeting of DGS facilities. Each DGS compound in Iraq has a prison, sometimes, as in Basra and al-Nasiriyya, in close proximity to the headquarters building. In both cases the United States was able to destroy the DGS headquarters buildings with little or no damage to the prisons. The United States apparently used penetrating weapons on each headquarters building and fired at an angle so that it would not spread damage to the prisons. The bombings also took place at night, offering further protection to the civilian population.

---

[116] Human Rights Watch interview with Dr. Rasmi al-Rikabi, director, Baghdad Red Crescent Maternity Hospital, Baghdad, May 22, 2003. The occupation of the Baghdad Red Crescent Maternity Hospital by the Iraqi Intelligence Service represents a clear breach of the Geneva Conventions. It is an abuse of the emblem of the red crescent. Though the hospital had been evacuated two weeks prior to the attack, it was still regarded as a medical facility and still looked like a hospital. For more information on this and other cases, see additional discussion in the Conduct of the Ground War chapter below.

[117] Human Rights Watch interview with Dr. Rasmi al-Rikabi.

Conclusion and Recommendations

The Coalition's record with preplanned targets in Iraq was mixed. It used precision-guided munitions and careful targeting to minimize civilian casualties in dozens of strikes on government buildings. U.S. attacks on alleged dual-use targets, however, were more controversial. Its destruction of media facilities was of questionable legality; Human Rights Watch found no evidence that the media was used to support Iraq's military effort. Coalition strikes on electrical power distribution facilities—although questionable military targets—demonstrate an attempt, through choice of weapons and targets, to reduce the effects on civilians, but the results still caused extensive civilian suffering.

Human Rights Watch recommends:

- Extreme caution be used in the targeting of electrical power facilities. In particular, electrical generation facilities should not be attacked at all. If electrical distribution facilities are attacked, it should be done in such a way as to cause only temporary incapacitation.

- Media installations not be attacked unless it is clear that they make an effective contribution to military action and their destruction offers a definite military advantage.

- Precision-guided munitions be used whenever possible, especially on targets in populated areas.

Cluster Bomb Strikes

While U.S. and U.K. air forces used primarily precision-guided munitions, they also dropped cluster bombs, which are notorious for causing harm to civilians.[118] Cluster munitions are large weapons that contain dozens and often hundreds of smaller submunitions. They can be air-launched or surface-delivered, releasing "bomblets" or "grenades" respectively. These weapons endanger civilians during strikes because they blanket a broad area with submunitions and are often inaccurate. They also leave large numbers of hazardous unexploded submunitions, or duds, that threaten civilians after the conflict. In Iraq, U.S. and U.K. use of cluster bombs caused civilian casualties both during strikes and afterwards. Their air forces for the most part demonstrated, however, that they had learned some of the lessons of past wars, notably in dropping far fewer

---

[118] For a more in-depth discussion of cluster munitions, see Human Rights Watch, "Fatally Flawed: Cluster Bombs and Their Use by the United States in Afghanistan," *A Human Rights Watch Report*, vol. 14, no. 7 (G), December 2002. For a complete list of Human Rights Watch documents on cluster munitions, see http://www.hrw.org/arms/clusterbombs.htm.

cluster bombs in populated areas. In contrast to Coalition ground forces, they significantly reduced the humanitarian harm of cluster strikes through better targeting and technology.

Introduction to Cluster Munitions

The military values cluster munitions because of their wide footprint and versatile submunitions. These munitions are area weapons that spread their contents over a large field, or footprint. Because of the dispersal of their submunitions, they can destroy broad, relatively soft targets, like airfields and surface-to-air missile sites. They are also effective against targets that move or do not have precise locations, such as enemy troops or vehicles. The submunitions themselves usually have multiple effects. Most of the models used in Iraq were both antipersonnel and anti-armor weapons.[119]

The military advantages of cluster munitions, however, must be weighed against their tendency to cause harm to civilians both during and after strikes. Most models, whether air-dropped or ground-launched, are unguided, and even those with guidance mechanisms are rarely precision guided. Unguided cluster munitions can miss their mark and hit nearby non-military objects. Once a cluster casing opens, it releases hundreds of submunitions that are also unguided[120] and disperse over a wide area.[121] Although other types of unguided weapons can miss their target, the humanitarian effects of a cluster accident are often more serious because of the submunitions' wide dispersal. Even if a cluster munition hits its target, the submunitions may kill civilians within the footprint. The inherent risks to civilian life and property increase when a party uses these weapons in or near populated areas. If cluster munitions are used in an area where combatants and civilians commingle, civilian casualties are almost assured.[122]

---

[119] Human Rights Watch, "Fatally Flawed," p. 7.

[120] The "skeets" of the CBU-105 are one exception to this rule. Used for the first time in Iraq, these warheads within a BLU-108 submunition are designed to guide themselves to armored vehicles. The new Sense and Destroy Armor Munitions (SADARM), artillery-launched submunitions, are another exception and operate in a similar way as the skeets.

[121] Because of the imprecision and the fact that submunitions do not always reliably explode, multiple cluster munitions with overlapping footprints are often used in attacks. The use of multiple weapons increases the potential area of destruction in strikes and produces more unexploded submunitions that have aftereffects. Colonel Lyle Cayce confirmed that the U.S. Army used such techniques in Iraq. He said the footprint of a round of six Multiple Launch Rocket System (MLRS) rockets could have a radius of .6 miles (one kilometer). Human Rights Watch telephone interview with Colonel Lyle Cayce, staff judge advocate, Third Infantry Division, U.S. Army, Washington, D.C., October 17, 2003.

[122] Human Rights Watch, "Fatally Flawed," p. 8.

Cluster munitions produce problematic aftereffects because many of the submunitions do not explode on impact as intended. While all weapons have a failure rate, cluster munitions are more dangerous because they release large numbers of submunitions and because certain design characteristics, based on cost and size considerations, increase the likelihood of submunitions' failure. As a result, every cluster munition leaves some unexploded ordnance. The dud, or initial failure, rate, i.e. the percentage that does not explode, not only reduces cluster munitions' military effectiveness but also puts civilians at great risk. Unexploded bomblets and grenades became *de facto* landmines that kill or injure civilians returning to the battle area after the attack.[123]

Coalition cluster munitions caused harm to civilians both during and after strikes in Iraq. This chapter and the next discuss the humanitarian impact of air and ground strikes, respectively. A third chapter discusses the aftereffects of cluster duds.

Cluster Bomb Strikes in the Iraq Air War

In three weeks from March 20 to April 9, U.S. and U.K. air forces dropped more cluster bombs in Iraq than they did in Afghanistan in six months. In Iraq, the United States used at least 1,206 clusters, containing more than 200,000 submunitions, only twenty-two shy of its half-year total for Afghanistan.[124] This number represents 4 percent of the total number of air-delivered weapons used by the Coalition. The U.S. Air Force used a wide variety of these bombs, including 818 CBU-103s, 182 CBU-99s, 118 CBU-87s, and 88 CBU-105s. The United States also deployed 253 AGM-154 Joint Stand Off Weapons (JSOWs) and 802 BGM-109 TLAMs, which can contain submunitions, but it did not report how many of those used in Iraq carried submunitions.[125] The side yard at the civil defense office in al-Hilla illustrated the breadth of the U.S. cluster arsenal. Clearance teams from this one city had collected pieces of cluster munitions delivered by planes and cruise missiles, as well as helicopters, artillery, and Multiple Launch Rocket Systems (MLRS). The array contrasts with Afghanistan where primarily CBU-87s and CBU-103s, different versions of the same bomb, were used. The United Kingdom contributed to the Coalition's cluster bomb use in Iraq. It dropped seventy RBL-755s, containing 147 submunitions each for a total of 10,290.[126]

---

[123] Ibid., pp. 8-9.

[124] This figure does not include two CBU-107s, which contain steel rods rather than explosive submunitions. "Operation Iraqi Freedom—By the Numbers," p. 11.

[125] Ibid.

[126] U.K. Ministry of Defence, "Operations in Iraq—First Reflections," July 2003, p. 24. In April, a member of parliament reported use of sixty-six RBL-755s. Hansard (House of Commons), April 30, 2003: col. 392W.

A clearance expert at al-Hilla Civil Defense Headquarters holds up two types of U.S. cluster submunitions used in Iraq. On the left is a ground-launched Dual-Purpose Improved Conventional Munition (DPICM), and on the right an air-dropped BLU-97. The duds he is holding were not dangerous because the fuzes and explosives had come out. © 2003 Bonnie Docherty / Human Rights Watch

The majority of the Coalition's cluster bombs were CBU-103s, which had been deployed for the first time in Afghanistan. This bomb consists of a three-part green metal casing about five-and-a-half feet (1.7 meters) long with a set of four fins attached to the rear. The casing, which contains 202 bomblets packed in yellow foam, opens at a pre-set altitude or time and releases the bomblets over a large oval area. The CBU-103 adds a Wind Corrected Munitions Dispenser (WCMD) to the rear of the unguided CBU-87, which is designed to improve accuracy by compensating for wind encountered during its fall. It also narrows the footprint to a radius of 600 feet (183 meters).[127]

The CBU-103's bomblets, known as BLU-97s, are soda can-sized yellow cylinders. Each one of these "combined effects munitions" represents a triple threat. The steel fragmentation core targets enemy troops with 300 jagged pieces of metal. The shaped charge, a concave copper cone that turns into a penetrating molten slug, serves as an anti-armor weapon. A zirconium wafer spreads incendiary fragments that can burn nearby vehicles.[128] This type of bomblet was the payload for 78 percent of the reported

---

[127] Human Rights Watch, "Fatally Flawed," pp. 6-7.

[128] Ibid.

U.S. cluster bombs; CBU-87s and CBU-103s both contain 202 BLUs. When used as cluster munitions, the AGM-154 JSOW contains 145 BLUs and the TLAM carries 166 BLUs.[129]

In Iraq, the Coalition used cluster bombs largely for their area effect and anti-armor capabilities. A CENTCOM official explained that common targets included armored vehicles or, when used with time-delay explosives, the path of thin-skinned vehicles.[130] "I know that some were used in more built-up areas, but in most cases they were used against targets where there were those kinds of equipment—guns, tanks," he said.[131] Human Rights Watch's field investigation supported these comments. Most of the cluster air strike sites it visited contained tanks, missiles, artillery, or thin-skinned vehicles. In a date grove in Hay Tunis, a neighborhood of Baghdad, Iraqis had hidden about a dozen military vehicles. The United States targeted it with both CBUs and unitary munitions. In Sichir, a small village outside al-Falluja, the United States dropped CBU-103s on a field with military vehicles protected by berms. Human Rights Watch found two casings and dozens of pieces of BLU debris at the adjacent chicken farm. In Agargouf, north of Baghdad, BLU duds were strewn across a field with SA-3 surface-to-air missiles and an accompanying radar truck. While military vehicles are legitimate targets, the impact of cluster bombs on civilians must still be considered.

The U.S. Air Force reduced the danger to civilians from clusters by modifying its targeting and improving technology. Apparently learning a lesson from previous conflicts, the Air Force dropped fewer cluster bombs in or near populated areas. While Human Rights Watch found extensive use of ground-launched cluster munitions in Iraq's cities, it found only isolated cases of air-dropped cluster bombs. As a result, the civilian casualties from cluster bomb strikes were relatively limited. According to a senior CENTCOM official, air commanders received guidance that one of their objectives was to minimize civilian casualties. "In the case of preplanned cluster munition strikes, I am more confident that concern for collateral damage was very high," he said.[132] Less care went into strikes on emerging targets in support of ground troops.

---

[129] The AGM-154A contains 145 BLUs; the AGM-154B contains six BLU-108/B submunitions, which will be described later in the discussion of CBU-105s. FAS [Federation of American Scientists] Military Analysis Network, "AGM-154A Joint Standoff Weapon [JSOW]," June 27, 2000, http://www.fas.org/man/dod-101/sys/smart/agm-154.htm (retrieved October 23, 2003). For information on the TLAM with submunitions, see Raytheon (General Dynamics), "Directory of U.S. Military Rockets and Missiles: AGM/BGM/RGM/UGM-109 Tomahawk," May 21, 2003, http://www.designation-systems.net/dusrm/m-109.html (retrieved October 23, 2003).

[130] Human Rights Watch telephone interview with senior CENTCOM official #2.

[131] Ibid.

[132] Ibid.

The CENTCOM official explained that B-52 bombers would carry a variety of munitions and loiter over the battlefield. If a ground commander called for support and cluster bombs were the only option left, the commander might accept them for his target. "As the battlefield unfolds and the sense of urgency on the ground goes up, my personal opinion is the urgency of the ground commander may be more for protection of his forces. Therefore choosing the optimal weapon is less important than getting a weapon on target," the official said.[133]

When the Air Force did not avoid populated areas, cluster bomb strikes caused civilian casualties. The Baghdad date grove was located immediately across the street, on at least two sides, from Hay Tunis, a densely populated, residential neighborhood. Nihad Salim Muhammad was washing his car when the bombs hit. During the strike, the bomblets injured several people on his street, including four children.[134] Around midnight on April 24, the U.S. Air Force dropped at least one CBU-103 on al-Hadaf girls' primary school in al-Hilla.[135] The strike killed school guard Hussam Hussain, 65, and neighbor Hamid Hamza, 45, and injured thirteen others, according to Hamid Mahdi, a 30-year-old butcher who lived across the street.[136] The manager of the school said there were dozens of paramilitary troops in the neighborhood at the time of the strike.[137] While the Air Force minimized civilian harm by dropping the bombs at night, the incident shows the dangers of dropping clusters in populated areas.

The Air Force also reduced the threat to civilians from cluster bomb strikes by using improved technology. The guided CBU-103, which is more accurate due to the WCMD, represented about 68 percent of the total number of reported cluster bombs used by the United States. Other cluster bombs with guidance systems included the CBU-105 and any JSOWs and TLAMs that carried submunitions. Such weapons choice is a dramatic improvement over that in the 1991 Gulf War and Yugoslavia, as well as Afghanistan, where the CBU-103 was introduced. In the latter conflict, use of older, unguided CBU-87s contributed to dozens of civilian deaths because they strayed from their targets and landed on nearby villages.[138] The WCMD technology probably contributed to the low

---

[133] Ibid.

[134] Human Rights Watch interview with Nihad Salim Muhammad, Baghdad, May 17, 2003.

[135] Human Rights Watch interview with Ibtisam Ibrahim Jassim, manager, al-Hadaf school, al-Hilla, May 20, 2003.

[136] Human Rights Watch interview with Hamid Mahdi, al-Hilla, May 20, 2003.

[137] Human Rights Watch interview with Ibtisam Ibrahim Jassim.

[138] Human Rights Watch, "Fatally Flawed," pp. 21-23.

An Iraqi girl sits in the playground of the pockmarked al-Hadaf primary school in al-Hilla. U.S. cluster bomblets killed two civilians and injured thirteen when they hit the school on April 24, 2003. © 2003 Marc Garlasco / Human Rights Watch

number of casualties in urban strikes like the ones in al-Hilla and Hay Tunis.[139] Given their location in the middle of urban areas, a less accurate weapon could have caused disastrous consequences. Despite the improved accuracy of the CBU-103, it is still not a precision-guided weapon, and the individual submunitions remain unguided and inaccurate. Militaries should not use cluster bombs in or near populated areas because their broad footprint and large number of bomblets make any error too deadly.

In addition to using the CBU-103 with WCMD, the U.S. Air Force took another major step toward increasing civilian protection by introducing the new CBU-105, or Sensor Fuzed Weapon. Similar to the CBU-87 and CBU-103 on the outside, this weapon contains ten BLU-108 submunitions that include four hockey puck-sized "skeets" each.

---

[139] Human Rights Watch confirmed the use of a CBU-103 in the strike on al-Hilla primary school because it found the casing at the site. It did not find a casing at the Hay Tunis site. It also found a CBU-103 casing in Sichir, a village near al-Falluja.

It has a WCMD, which guides the casing, and, more importantly, an infrared guidance system on each skeet that directs it to armored vehicles.[140]

Despite some improvements in technology, one of the Coalition's major failings with cluster bombs was use of outdated cluster bombs. Both the United States and United Kingdom continued to drop older models that are highly inaccurate and unreliable. In addition to unguided CBU-87s, the United States used 182 Vietnam-era CBU-99 Rockeyes, containing 247 Mk-118 submunitions.[141] The United Kingdom used seventy RBL-755s, similar to the Rockeye but with 147 submunitions.[142] Rockeyes, which were developed in the 1950s, were used in great numbers in the Vietnam War and 1991 Gulf War. Such outdated stockpiles should not be used, especially now that the Coalition has technology that can reduce the civilian casualties caused by cluster bomb strikes.[143]

Conclusion and Recommendations

The immediate effects of cluster bombs, i.e. the damage done during strikes, may in certain cases be indiscriminate because the weapons cannot be precisely targeted. International humanitarian law prohibits attacks "which employ a method or means of combat which cannot be directed at a specific military objective."[144] Bombings that treat "separated and distinct" military objectives as one are also expressly prohibited.[145] Cluster bombs are area weapons, useful in part for attacking dispersed or moving targets. They cannot, however, be directed at specific soldiers or tanks, a limitation that is particularly troublesome in populated areas. The principle that multiple targets should not be treated as one supports the argument that cluster bombs should not be used in populated areas.

As stated above, an attack is disproportionate, and thus indiscriminate, if it "may be expected to cause incidental loss of civilian life, injury to civilians, damage to civilian objects, or a combination thereof, which would be excessive in relation to the concrete

---

[140] "CBU-97/B Sensor Fuzed Weapon System (SFW) (with BLU-108)," *Jane's Air-Launched Weapons*, ed. Duncan Lennox (Surrey, U.K.: Jane's Information Group, 1999).

[141] "Operation Iraqi Freedom—By the Numbers," p. 11. For information on the Rockeye, see ORDATA Online, "U.S. Bomb, Guided, Rockeye Munition (GRM)," February 4, 2002, http://maic.jmu.edu/ordata/srdetaildesc.asp?ordid=391 (retrieved October 24, 2003).

[142] U.K. Ministry of Defence, "Operations in Iraq—First Reflections."

[143] Human Rights Watch, "Cluster Munitions a Foreseeable Hazard in Iraq," *A Human Rights Watch Briefing Paper*, March 2003.

[144] Protocol I, art. 51(4)(b).

[145] Ibid., art. 51(5)(a).

and direct military advantage anticipated."[146] Some kinds of cluster bomb attacks tend to tip the scale toward being disproportionate. While Human Rights Watch neither has the information nor is in a position to evaluate the military advantages expected from the cluster bomb attacks, it is nevertheless concerned about the significant civilian casualties these attacks caused.

An August 2001 U.S. Air Force background paper acknowledges that cluster munitions "must pass [the] proportionality test" and states that there are "[c]learly some areas where CBUs normally couldn't be used (e.g. populated city centers)."[147] The definition of a populated area should include not only cities but also villages and their environs.[148] Based on research in Iraq, Afghanistan, and Yugoslavia, Human Rights Watch believes that when cluster bombs are used in any type of populated area, there should be a strong, if rebuttable, presumption under the proportionality test that an attack is indiscriminate.

In Iraq, the U.S. Air Force took steps to reduce humanitarian harm by using newer, guided cluster bombs and generally avoiding populated areas. Human Rights Watch did not find many examples of urban strikes, but any that did happen would have to be evaluated on a case-by-case basis for compliance with IHL. As will be shown in the next chapter, the use of ground-launched submunitions is a very different story.

Human Rights Watch has since 1999 called for a suspension of cluster bomb use until the weapon's humanitarian effects have been fully addressed.[149] If armed forces do use cluster bombs, Human Rights Watch recommends the following to minimize civilian casualties during cluster air strikes:

---

[146] Ibid., art. 51(5)(b).

[147] U.S. Air Force, Bullet Background Paper on International Legal Aspects Concerning the Use of Cluster Munitions, August 30, 2001. This is an informal paper prepared by the office of the Air Force Judge Advocate General.

[148] The Convention on Conventional Weapons (CCW), for example, defines "concentrations of civilians" as "any concentration of civilians, be it permanent or temporary, such as inhabited parts of cities, or inhabited towns or villages. . . ." Convention on Prohibitions or Restrictions on the Use of Certain Conventional Weapons Which May Be Deemed to Be Excessively Injurious or to Have Indiscriminate Effects, Protocol III (Prohibitions or Restrictions on the Use of Incendiary Weapons), 1980, amended December 21, 2001, art. 1(2).

[149] Human Rights Watch, Cluster Bombs: Memorandum for Convention on Conventional Weapons (CCW) Delegates, December 16, 1999.

- Armed forces should cease use of old, unguided and unreliable cluster bombs, such as the Rockeye, CBU-87, and RBL-755.

- Armed forces should not use cluster bombs in or near populated areas.

III. CONDUCT OF THE GROUND WAR

The hostilities in Iraq in March and April 2003 were the largest engagement of ground forces since the Gulf War in 1991. The U.S.-led Coalition deployed about 350,000 ground forces,[150] while the Iraqis fought with an estimated 350,000 ground forces in the regular army and Republican Guard[151] and between 18,000 and 40,000 paramilitary fedayeen.[152] Human Rights Watch documented a number of cases that constituted serious violations of IHL by Iraqi armed forces. Despite taking extensive precautions to protect civilians, U.S. and U.K. ground forces were found to have caused significant numbers of civilian casualties with the widespread use of cluster munitions, particularly in populated areas. Moreover, in some instances of direct combat, problems with training on as well as dissemination and clarity of the U.S. ground forces' rules of engagement may have, in some instances, contributed to loss of civilian life.

Synopsis of the Ground War

On March 20, 2003, at approximately 6:15 p.m. local time, artillery from the U.S. Army's Third Infantry Division fired upon targets inside Iraq, followed shortly thereafter by artillery from the U.S. Marine Corps' First Marine Division. By nightfall, mechanized infantry and armored forces from the Third Infantry Division, First Marine Division, and the British Army's First Armoured Division had crossed the Iraq-Kuwait border. The U.S. Marines and British forces headed toward Umm Qasr, al-Fao Peninsula, and Basra, while the Third Infantry Division took a more westerly route to the Euphrates River Valley and, ultimately, to Baghdad.[153]

---

[150] "Operation Iraqi Freedom—By the Numbers," p. 3. This number includes all "deployed personnel," not just combat troops.

[151] "State of the Iraqi Military," *New York Times*, n.d., http://www.wfaa.com/sharedcontent/dallas/graphics/10-02/0826int_iraq_military.pdf (retrieved October 20, 2003).

[152] The Fedayeen Saddam are paramilitary forces that have strong political loyalty to Saddam Hussein and, before the war, reported directly to the presidential palace rather than through the regular army's command. The term "fedayeen" is also sometimes used to refer to opposition forces from other Arab countries, particularly Syria, that came to Iraq to fight the Coalition in this war. See Global Security.org, "Saddam's Martyrs ['Men of Sacrifice']: *Fedayeen* Saddam," n.d., http://www.globalsecurity.org/intell/world/iraq/fedayeen.htm (retrieved October 20, 2003). The proper transliteration of "fedayeen" is fida'iyyin, with the singular being fida'i, but Human Rights Watch has used the more common spelling to refer to singular and plural combatants in this report.

[153] Steven Lee Myers, "G.I.'s and Marines See Little Iraqi Resistance," *New York Times*, March 21, 2003, p. B4.

Coalition forces seized Umm Qasr by March 21, though skirmishes continued outside the city. British forces and elements of the First Marine Division encircled Basra on March 22. While British forces settled in to probe Basra's defenses and cut off the city, the First Marine Division pushed northwest along the Euphrates River toward al-Nasiriyya. Task Force Tarawa, the Marines' lead element, encountered Iraqi forces on the outskirts of al-Nasiriyya just before dawn on March 23, 2003.[154] A pitched battle between U.S. Marines and Iraqi forces ensued in and around the city for several days. Some of the bloodiest fighting of the war occurred along a stretch of highway in al-Nasiriyya that became known as "Ambush Alley." Having pushed through al-Nasiriyya by March 31, Marine units conducted raids on Ba`th party headquarters in the town of al-Shatra.[155] The First Marine Division then moved toward the city of al-Kut on the Tigris River. By April 2, U.S. forces were positioned to assault Baghdad from the southeast.

Meanwhile, advance elements of the Third Infantry Division pushed as far as one hundred miles (160 kilometers) inside Iraq by the evening of March 21.[156] On March 22, the division's Second Brigade engaged enemy forces in al-Samawa, southeast of al-Najaf, while its Third Brigade seized a key bridge across the Euphrates River just northwest of al-Nasiriyya. It also captured al-Talil airbase, southwest of that city and next to the ruins of the ancient city of Ur.[157] The First Brigade moved the farthest of the three units, reaching a wide, flat desert plain known as the "Sea of al-Najaf" on the outskirts of the city of al-Najaf. By March 23, the Third Infantry Division had advanced nearly two-thirds of the distance from the Kuwait border to Baghdad.[158] In their rapid advance northward, elements of the division avoided fighting in the cities of al-Nasiriyya, al-Samawa, and al-Najaf, leaving behind pockets of resistance. By the time the Third Infantry Division was just north of al-Najaf, its lines of supply and communication extended more than 300 miles (482 kilometers) to the Kuwaiti border and were vulnerable to attack from the regular and irregular Iraqi units that the Americans had passed en route. Hampered by fierce sandstorms beginning on March 25 and stiff

---

[154] Michael Wilson, "Marines Meet Potent Enemy in Deadly Fight," *New York Times*, March 24, 2003, p. A1.

[155] Rajiv Chandrasekaran and Alan Sipress, "Army Has First Close Clashes with Republican Guard Units; Iraqi Divisions Shifted South to Defend Capital," *Washington Post*, April 1, 2003, p. A1.

[156] Patrick Tyler, "Surrenders by Iraqi Forces; 2 Marines Die in Fighting," *New York Times*, March 22, 2003, p. A1.

[157] Patrick Tyler, "Capital Hit Again; Invading Forces Capture Key Bridge; More American Deaths," *New York Times*, March 23, 2003.

[158] Steven Lee Myers, "Closing in on Baghdad, U.S. Troops Batter Iraqis," *New York Times*, March 24, 2003, p. B4.

resistance from irregular forces around al-Samawa and al-Najaf, U.S. forces halted their advance to consolidate supply lines and eliminate Iraqi forces.

During this pause, U.S. Air Force, Navy, and Army tactical aircraft continued to attack Republican Guard divisions south of Baghdad. Between April 1 and 2, the First Marine Division began to progress up Highway 7 toward al-Kut.[159] Nearly simultaneously, the U.S. Army began to push through the Karbala' Gap.[160] U.S. forces advanced toward Baghdad from the southeast and the southwest in a coordinated movement, while elements of the 101st and 82nd Airborne Divisions stayed behind to pacify al-Najaf and Karbala' after major fighting there. The First Brigade of the Third Infantry Division began the battle for the Saddam International Airport on April 4 while the Second Brigade assumed a blocking position to the south of the city; the First Marine Division approached to within ten miles (sixteen kilometers) of Baghdad from the southeast and spread over an arc to the east of the city.[161]

On April 5, the Second Brigade of the Third Infantry Division made the first U.S. foray into downtown Baghdad with a column of sixty armored vehicles. After a three-hour movement through the city, it withdrew to its staging area to the south of Baghdad.[162] On April 7, the brigade made another thrust, this time through the governmental district to the Republican Palace complex, and stayed overnight in Baghdad. These operations on April 5 and 7 were nicknamed "Thunder Run." On April 7, Basra fell to British forces.[163] On April 9, Baghdad fell to U.S. forces.[164]

Iraqi Conduct in the Ground War

Iraqi forces violated international humanitarian law during the ground war, directly causing or contributing to civilian casualties. In particular, Human Rights Watch documented instances of abuse of the red cross and red crescent emblems; violations of the prohibitions on the use of civilian shields, use of antipersonnel landmines, and location of military objects in protected places, such as hospitals, mosques, and cultural property sites; and a failure to take precautions in preparing for urban combat.

---

[159] John Kifner, "Orders in Place, Word Goes Out that 'This is It,'" *New York Times*, April 1, 2003, p. B7.

[160] Steven Lee Myers, "G.I.'s Pry Iraqis Loose and Surge Over River," *New York Times*, April 3, 2003, p. A1.

[161] Patrick Tyler, "U.S. Squeezes Baghdad," *New York Times*, April 6, 2003.

[162] Patrick Tyler, "Show of Force," *New York Times*, April 6, 2003.

[163] Craig Smith, "Basra Falls, Though Fighting Persists," *New York Times*, April 8, 2003.

[164] Patrick Tyler, "Combat; U.S. Forces Take Control in Baghdad; Bush Elated; Some Resistance Remains," *New York Times*, April 10, 2003, p. A1.

Witnesses also reported large numbers of Iraqi soldiers wearing civilian clothes, a practice that eroded the distinction between combatant and civilian and put the latter at risk. It must be noted that Human Rights Watch was unable to interview members of the Iraqi armed forces in order to get their response to accusations of violations of IHL.

Use of Human Shields

According to Human Rights Watch interviewees and U.S. and U.K. media reports, Iraqi armed forces endangered civilians by using them to shield combatants from the enemy. Iraqi prisoners of war said they received orders to "use any means necessary" during their battle with the Marines including "putting women and children in the street."[165] Human Rights Watch gathered testimonies that are consistent with such allegations. Yusif Sahib Jawad, a 29-year-old taxi driver, witnessed fedayeen fighters hiding between houses on al-Madina Street where much of the fighting in al-Najaf took place. "Most of the fedayeen and Ba`thists distributed and hid between houses because they thought the Americans wouldn't shoot civilians. They used civilians as shields," he said.[166] In one case, he saw Ba`th militia members spot a U.S. helicopter in the sky and then pull their car next to a car carrying a civilian family. The helicopter fired and seven civilians died in their vehicle, Jawad said.[167] The press reported that helicopter pilots often encountered these kinds of situations.[168]

Coalition forces interviewed by Human Rights Watch reported other cases of the use of human shields that they had witnessed. In al-Najaf, Colonel David Perkins, commanding officer of the Second Brigade, Third Infantry Division, saw a fedayeen drive behind a home in a four-by-four vehicle with its lights off. "He went into the building, came out with two women, one was holding a child. So everyone held their fire, and luckily the women were able to break loose," Perkins said. After his hostages fled, the fedayeen jumped back in his vehicle and started shooting; the U.S. troops then killed him.[169] Perkins witnessed another case as his unit was trying to take a bridge

---

[165] Kerry Sanders, "Iraqis Deceive Marines at al-Nasiriyya: Men in Civilian Clothes Ambush U.S. Soldiers on Key Bridges," MSNBC News, March 24, 2003, http://www.msnbc.com/news/890065.asp (retrieved October 17, 2003).

[166] Human Rights Watch interview with Yusif Sahib Jawad, al-Najaf, May 24, 2003.

[167] Ibid.

[168] Dexter Filkins, "Choosing Targets; Iraqi Fighters or Civilians? Hard Decision for Copters," *New York Times*, March 31, 2003. Filkins quoted several U.S. helicopter pilots who said Iraqi soldiers would fire and then disappear in a crowd of civilians before the helicopters could respond. Corporal Joshua Good, for example, said, "I may be 99 percent sure of the guy who shot at me, but if I fly back around and he doesn't have a gun and he is standing with a bunch of women and children, then I can't fire."

[169] Human Rights Watch interview with Colonel David Perkins.

across the Euphrates. Iraqi forces lined up civilians in front of their vehicles so they could advance safely. "It would cease all fire," Perkins said.[170] A sergeant in Perkins' brigade said that during the battle of Baghdad, fedayeen would use civilians to shield themselves while running across the street.[171]

Members of other service branches reported similar situations. Major Michael Samarov, a battalion executive officer, encountered civilian shields as his Marines entered Baghdad on April 8. "There were busloads of people driven to our position on Highway 6. When [the Iraqi military advance] wouldn't work, they threw families in the vehicles. It was a very challenging situation. We made every attempt to minimize casualties, but it was extraordinarily difficult," he said.[172] In al-Shatra, a Marine corporal said a caravan of three buses drove toward his unit. Fedayeen had put women and children in the first two to allow the third carrying fedayeen to advance on the Marines safely.[173] British troops also reported shielding from the southern part of the country. During fighting east of Basra, Colonel Gil Baldwin, commanding officer of the Queen's Dragoon Guards, said he saw Iraqi forces "herd" women and children out of their homes and fire rocket-propelled grenades (RPGs) over their heads.[174] Human Rights Watch could not corroborate these specific incidents with non-military sources; however, the detail and repetition of the reports suggests a pattern.

The U.S. and U.K. press also reported incidents of Iraqi forces using civilians, including children, as human shields. In one of many accounts, Sergeant David Baird, a tank commander of the Royal Scots Dragoon Guards, said fedayeen "were crossing the road to try and outflank us on the left and, as they crossed, four or five of them grabbed kids by the scruff of their necks and dragged them across with them. . . . The children were only five to eight years old." After the fedayeen crossed, they let the children run back to their mothers.[175]

---

[170] Ibid.

[171] Human Rights Watch interview with Sergeant First Class Morales, Second Brigade, Third Infantry Division, U.S. Army, Baghdad, May 18, 2003.

[172] Human Rights Watch interview with Major Michael Samarov, executive officer, Third Battalion, Seventh Marines, U.S. Marine Corps, Karbala', May 25, 2003.

[173] Human Rights Watch interview with U.S. Marine corporal, al-Hilla, May 20, 2003.

[174] Human Rights Watch telephone interview with Colonel Gil Baldwin, commanding officer, First Queen's Dragoon Guards, Cardiff, Wales, July 2, 2003.

[175] Martin Bentham, "Iraqi Paramilitaries 'Used Children as Human Shields,'" *Independent*, April 2, 2003. See also Dexter Filkins, "Choosing Targets; Iraqi Fighters or Civilians? Hard Decision for Copters" (describing how "Iraqi soldiers try to blend in or hide behind civilians after shooting at the Americans"); Jules Crittenden, "'We Weren't Expecting This'; Iraq's Civilian Ploys Force Deadly Decisions," *Boston Herald*, April 2, 2003 (quoting an

International humanitarian law prohibits the use of civilians as shields. Parties to a conflict are expressly prohibited from directing the movement of civilians to attempt to shield military objectives from attacks or to shield military operations.[176] In the cases described above, Iraqi soldiers used civilian bystanders to do both of the prohibited activities: to protect themselves and to advance on their enemy.

Abuse of Red Cross and Red Crescent Emblems

Iraqi armed forces violated international humanitarian law by abusing the red cross and red crescent emblems. These emblems may only be used to identify and protect medical personnel, buildings, and equipment in times of armed conflict and to identify national Red Cross and Red Crescent societies, the International Committee of the Red Cross (ICRC), and the International Federation of Red Cross and Red Crescent Societies.

The night of March 23, during the battle for al-Najaf, fedayeen came to the Hay al-Hussain Ambulance Center. The ambulances there and in other parts of Iraq were white with red crescent emblems on the front hood and rear door and sometimes on the side door. The fedayeen told the center's staff that they knew of injured people who needed help and climbed in an ambulance with their guns. "They got in . . . and then took part in the battle. They used [the ambulance] as a cover to reach the field of battle," said Rashid Majid Hamid, 42, a paramedic, who witnessed two such cases.[177] At 11:00 p.m. five days later, an intelligence official commandeered an ambulance from the same center and posed as an ambulance driver to scout the road twenty kilometers (12.4 miles) southeast of al-Najaf. Paramedic Falah Muhsin, 52, said he was afraid to go along but "had no choice."[178] While these examples involved taking local ambulances, in other cases, the fedayeen took ambulances from a more central source. "Because they have so much power, they take them from the Ministry of Health," Muhsin said.[179] A doctor at al-Najaf Teaching Hospital said he saw fedayeen driving in cars with red crescent

---

intelligence specialist saying, "We've seen them pull women and children into buildings so the Americans won't shoot."); Dana Lewis, "Iraqis Ambush American Tanks," MSNBC News, April 1, 2003, http://www.msnbc.com/news/894006.asp (retrieved October 17, 2003) ("Iraqi soldiers used women and children as human shields").

[176] Protocol I, art. 51(7).

[177] Human Rights Watch interview with Rashid Majid Hamid, paramedic, Hay al-Hussain Ambulance Center, al-Najaf, May 24, 2003.

[178] Human Rights Watch interview with Falah Muhsin, paramedic, Hay al-Hussain Ambulance Center, al-Najaf, May 24, 2003.

[179] Ibid.

flags.[180] Coalition troops confirmed they had come under attack from ambulances. Major Samarov said the Marines took fire from ambulances one or two nights.[181] In another instance of abuse of the red crescent emblem, the Iraqi Intelligence Service occupied the Red Crescent Maternity Hospital in Baghdad.[182]

An international aid worker also told Human Rights Watch that Iraqi forces disguised a Ba`th party militia building in Basra, with no connection to the ICRC, by affixing an ICRC emblem to it before the war started.[183] Such buildings served as rallying points for the local militia. They were used to store small arms, ammunition, rockets, grenades, and other ordnance, and during a crisis, the militia would go to there to receive orders.

These actions violate the prohibition on abuse of the emblem. International humanitarian law has long prohibited making improper use of the "distinctive emblem" of the red cross or red crescent.[184] Attacking the enemy under cover of the red crescent constitutes an abuse of the emblem. Using the ICRC emblem to protect military objects is equally unlawful.

Use of Antipersonnel Landmines

Iraqi forces violated the prohibition on the use of indiscriminate weapons by laying antipersonnel landmines in several parts of the country. British Royal Marines advancing toward Basra encountered freshly sown antipersonnel minefields as well as newly laid antivehicle mines that slowed their progress.[185] "The U.N. withdrew three or four days before the war. Then the Iraqis rushed to put mines along the border," said Dr. Akram al-Shuwali, director of Umm Qasr General Hospital.[186] Mines caused several of the civilian casualties his hospital received during the war.[187] Further north, Iraqi

---

[180] Human Rights Watch interview with Dr. `Ali al-Tufaili, director, al-Najaf General Hospital, May 24, 2003.

[181] Human Rights Watch interview with Major Michael Samarov. See also Jules Crittenden, "'We Weren't Expecting This'; Iraq's Civilian Ploys Force Deadly Decisions" (quoting an intelligence sergeant saying, "They are using ambulances to carry troops and resupply. They jump out blazing.").

[182] Human Rights Watch interview with Dr. Rasmi al-Rikabi.

[183] Human Rights Watch interview with international aid worker #1, Basra, April 30, 2003.

[184] Protocol I, art. 38.

[185] Tim Butcher, "Marines Plan the Siege of Basra," *Daily Telegraph*, March 31, 2003.

[186] Human Rights Watch interview with Dr. Akram al-Shuwali, director, Umm Qasr General Hospital, Umm Qasr, May 28, 2003.

[187] Ibid. See also Lawrence M. O'Rourke, "Conflict with Iraq: Fedayeen Could Pose Lingering Threat, Aid Worker Says," *Naples Daily News*, April 5, 2003.

forces used landmines against advancing U.S. troops. Landmines newly planted prior to the Coalition attack were reported on the road between Basra and Baghdad.[188] The Iraqis reportedly deployed landmines along access routes to their positions around al Nasiriyya.[189] U.S. troops entering al-Najaf in the last days of March encountered mines on roads and bridges into the city.[190] The Third Infantry Division was also "held up in a minefield" near Karbala'.[191] According to a U.S. State Department demining expert, most mines found were a twenty-year-old design, largely imported from Italy.[192]

Although the heaviest fighting took place in south and central Iraq, Iraqi forces also used mines north of Baghdad. In March 2003, reports emerged of Iraqi forces laying mines around the northern city of Kirkuk.[193] It was confirmed after the Iraqi forces withdrew that they had laid antipersonnel and antivehicle landmines in dense minefields along and between main roads near Kirkuk and around abandoned military posts.[194] Demining teams from the Mines Advisory Group operating in Kirkuk found Valmara 69 antipersonnel bounding fragmentation mines and PMN antipersonnel blast mines placed across nearly all routes and around strategic points.[195] Mines were also encountered on the roads between Erbil and the cities of Kirkuk, Gwer, Mosul, and Makhmur.[196]

Iraqis used landmines not only along their borders and the route of advancing enemy troops but also around civilian infrastructure. "One month ago, the power lines were down and we could only get to the building through a minefield," said Lieutenant Colonel John Shanahan, commanding officer of a British explosive ordnance disposal

---

[188] "U.S. Landmine Experts Begin Removal Work in Iraq," Voice of America, May 24, 2003.

[189] "Russian Military Intel Update: War in Iraq, March 25, 2003," *War in Iraq*, March 25, 2003, http://www.iraqwar.ru/iraq-read_article.php?articleId=729&lang=en (retrieved November 6, 2003). This document is a translation of a Russian military intelligence report done by Venik.

[190] "Iraq Stored Landmines in Mosque," Reuters, April 3, 2003 (citing *New York Times*).

[191] Human Rights Watch interview with Major Michael Samarov.

[192] "U.S. Landmine Experts Begin Removal Work in Iraq."

[193] "U.S. and Britain Struggle to Find Iraq Consensus," Reuters, March 11, 2003; "Iraqi Forces Litter Northern Front with Landmines," Agence France-Presse, March 19, 2003.

[194] Mines Advisory Group, "MAG in Iraq—First in, Last out," ReliefWeb, April 19, 2003, http://www.reliefweb.int/w/rwb.nsf/0/d28473fd37debf46c1256d1d0032c01?OpenDocument (retrieved October 21, 2003).

[195] Ibid.

[196] Muhy-al-Din Qadr, "Over 1,000 Mines Removed from Just Three Liberated Areas," *Brayati* (Iraqi Kurdistan Democratic Party), April 26, 2003, republished as "Over 1,000 Mines Removed in April—Kurdish Paper," BBC, April 28, 2003.

(EOD) unit in Basra.[197] British troops near the southern al-Rumaila oilfields found mines and booby-traps left by Iraqi forces.[198] As part of their widespread mine-laying around villages in the Mosul-Kirkuk area, Iraqi forces reportedly mined water tanks in the town of Chamchamal after cutting off its water supply. [199] Regardless of location, Iraqi mines continued to endanger civilians after the war. In May, Human Rights Watch found abandoned Iraqi weapons caches that included antipersonnel mines and learned about both caches and minefields from clearance technicians in Basra, Karbala', al-Hilla, and Baghdad.[200]

Human Rights Watch believes that the use of antipersonnel landmines is prohibited by customary international law because they are inherently indiscriminate weapons.[201] International humanitarian law prohibits "a method or means of combat which cannot be directed at a specific military objective."[202] Antipersonnel landmines fall into that category. They cannot distinguish between combatants, legitimate military objectives, and civilians who inadvertently activate them. Thus, even though Iraq is not among the 141 parties to the 1997 Mine Ban Treaty that prohibits use, production, transfer, and stockpiling of antipersonnel mines,[203] Human Rights Watch considers any use of such mines by Iraq a violation of IHL.

Location of Military Objectives in Protected Places

In addition to protecting civilians, international humanitarian law gives special protection to certain facilities, including hospitals, places of worship, and cultural property. Iraqi armed forces used these protected places to advance their military goals. The fedayeen, for example, used al-Nasiriyya Surgical Hospital as the base of their local operations.[204]

---

[197] Human Rights Watch interview with Lieutenant Colonel John Shanahan, commanding officer, Joint Forces EOD Team, 33 Engineers Regiment, Corps of Royal Engineers, British Army, Basra, May 28, 2003.

[198] Lindsay Taylor, "Basra and Baghdad," Channel 4 News (U.K.), March 25, 2003, http://www.channel4.com/news/2003/03/week_4/25_war.html (retrieved October 21, 2003).

[199] Michael Holden, "Iraqis Face 'Horrendous' Mine Legacy," Reuters, April 3, 2003.

[200] Human Rights Watch interview with Lieutenant Colonel John Shanahan; Human Rights Watch interview with Gunnery Sergeant Tracey Jones, EOD team leader, Brigade Service Support Group 1, U.S. Marine Corps, Karbala', May 25, 2003; Human Rights Watch interview with Lieutenant Jerry Roeder, First Battalion, Fourth Marines, U.S. Marine Corps, al-Hilla, May 20, 2003.

[201] See Protocol I, art. 51(4).

[202] Ibid., art. 51(4)(b).

[203] Convention on the Prohibition of the Use, Stockpiling, Production, and Transfer of Anti-Personnel Mines and on Their Destruction, September 18, 1997. This convention is also known as the "Mine Ban Treaty."

[204] Human Rights Watch interview with Dr. `Ali `Abd al-Sayyid, director, al-Nasiriyya General Hospital, May 7, 2003.

As discussed above, the *Mukhabarat* occupied the Baghdad Red Crescent Maternity Hospital and threatened to kill Dr. al-Rikabi, the hospital director, if he challenged them.[205] Such military use of civilian hospitals violates international humanitarian law. Parties to an armed conflict are required to respect and protect civilian hospitals, which may in no circumstances be attacked.[206] This protection ceases, however, if the medical establishments are used to commit "acts harmful to the enemy."[207] By using hospitals as military headquarters, Iraqi forces turned them into military objectives.

Iraqi armed forces also sought to protect themselves by establishing positions in mosques. In al-Najaf, they occupied the Imam `Ali Mosque, the most holy religious site in Iraq. Wasfi Tahir, a 26-year-old merchant, said he saw Iraqi fedayeen and Ba`th militia fighting from this mosque in the middle of the city. He said the fedayeen fired at U.S. troops, but the Americans did not return fire.[208] The press reported that about 150 members of the Ba`th party and Fedayeen Saddam had taken positions in the mosque.[209] In Baghdad, fedayeen from Syria moved into the Abu Hanifa mosque, one of the holiest Sunni shrines in Iraq. At 4:00 a.m. on April 9, a firefight broke out between U.S. forces and fedayeen inside the mosque. According to a fedayeen combatant, the battle lasted until around noon, killing ten civilians and causing significant damage to the mosque's well-known clock tower.[210]

International humanitarian law prohibits the use of "places of worship which constitute the cultural or spiritual heritage of peoples . . . in support of the military effort."[211] The Imam `Ali and Abu Hanifa mosques are not only places of worship, but also mosques with special religious and historical significance to Shi`a and Sunni Muslims, respectively. Iraqi forces' use of these mosques for military actions is clearly illegal.

---

[205] Human Rights Watch interview with Dr. Rasmi al-Rikabi.

[206] Fourth Geneva Convention, art. 18.

[207] Ibid., art. 19.

[208] Human Rights Watch interview with Wasfi Tahir, al-Najaf, May 24, 2003.

[209] Scott Fornek, "Troops Blast Baghdad; Bush: 'We Will Now Go the Last 200 Yards,'" *Chicago Sun-Times*, April 4, 2003. See also "The Conduct of the War," Voice of America, transcript, April 4, 2003.

[210] Human Rights Watch interview with fedayeen, Baghdad, May 18, 2003. This fedayeen, 45, participated in the battle and was injured although he did not go to the hospital for fear of being turned in.

[211] Protocol I, art. 53(b).

Fedayeen from Syria occupied the Abu Hanifa mosque in Baghdad, and on April 9, a firefight broke out between U.S. forces and fedayeen inside the mosque. Damage to the mosque's clock tower is visible in this photo. © 2003 Bonnie Docherty / Human Rights Watch

Iraqi forces also endangered cultural property by establishing military positions around historical landmarks. Agargouf is a fifteenth-century B.C. ziggurat. Ghanan Fadhil, an archaeologist at the site, said the Iraqi military had placed rocket launchers around the site and anti-aircraft guns on top of the mud-brick temple. They also occupied the museum restaurant, only a couple hundred yards from the ziggurat. The Coalition attacked these forces with both air- and ground-launched cluster munitions. "They didn't hit the ziggurat but the site was so close there were many cracks in newer unsettled places," Fadhil said.[212] When Human Rights Watch visited Agargouf in May, it found an SA-3 surface-to-air missile site across the road, a restaurant that had been trashed, and bullet shell casings on top of the monument. This kind of collocation violates the prohibition on use of "historic monuments . . . which constitute the cultural or spiritual heritage of peoples . . . in support of the military effort."[213]

Lack of Precautions in Preparing for Urban Combat

Iraqi forces regularly located military equipment in heavily populated areas. Human Rights Watch saw military vehicles or anti-aircraft positions in schools and residential

---

[212] Human Rights Watch interview with Ghanan Fadhil, curator, Agargouf ziggurat, Agargouf, May 17, 2003.

[213] Protocol I, art. 53(b).

neighborhoods in every city it visited. In at least some cases, the placement of this military hardware suggested that Iraqi armed forces failed to take the necessary precautions to spare civilians from the dangers of urban warfare.

From Baghdad to Basra, Human Rights Watch documented dozens of examples of such lack of precautions. Iraqi forces established positions in civilian areas in the weeks before the war. They brought military vehicles and weapons into Nadir, a crowded slum in al-Hilla, a week or so before the conflict began and several weeks before the battle there.[214] In a village on the road between al-Hilla and Baghdad, Human Rights Watch saw three tanks wedged into three narrow alleyways. Such placement would not have been the result of ordinary maneuvers during battle. At al-Najah Intermediary School for Girls, located in a Karbala' residential area, Iraqi troops had dug fighting positions with anti-aircraft guns in the schoolyard.[215] Human Rights Watch found dug-in mortar positions and anti-aircraft cannons between homes in Hay al-Zaitun in Basra. Such placements appear to have been intentional, not merely the result of falling back into urban areas during fighting.

Iraqi forces also placed large caches of weapons and ammunition in civilian neighborhoods. For example, residents said troops established caches in Hay al-Khadra, a neighborhood of Baghdad, the week before the war started.[216] Several munition stores seemed to pre-date the war. Human Rights Watch visited a huge storage facility near al-Maqal Airfield in Basra that was only a half-kilometer (.3 miles) from a civilian neighborhood. The quantity and nature of the munitions stored at this facility were such that if it had been attacked, the civilian neighborhood would have suffered extensive damage. These caches and the dangers they have posed to civilians are addressed in the last chapter of this report.

---

[214] Human Rights Watch interview with Talib Madhlum `Abdullah, al-Hilla, October 13, 2003; Human Rights Watch interview with Ahmad Khalaf Jabbar, al-Hilla, October 13, 2003; Human Rights Watch interview with `Adil Sa`ad al-Shami, al-Hilla, October 13, 2003; Human Rights Watch interview with `Ali Hassan Fakhr, al-Hilla, October 13, 2003.

[215] Human Rights Watch found additional evidence of occupation of schools in Baghdad, al-Hilla, al-Najaf, and Basra.

[216] Human Rights Watch interview with Munkith Fathi `Abd al-Razzaq, Baghdad, October 10, 2003; Human Rights Watch interview with Haidar Majed Suhail and Hazza` Majed Suhail, Baghdad, October 10, 2003; Human Rights Watch interview with Muhammad Salih Mahdi, Baghdad, October 10, 2003.

Iraqi forces placed this anti-aircraft gun in the yard of al-Najah Intermediary School for Girls, located in a Karbala' residential area. It was one of dozens of examples of Iraqi placement of military hardware in civilian neighborhoods. © 2003 Bonnie Docherty / Human Rights Watch

Some Iraqi civilians interviewed by Human Rights Watch interpreted the location of military hardware in neighborhoods as an intentional attempt by the Iraqi armed forces to use civilians to protect military objectives. "They put anti-aircraft guns in civilian parts to have a safe place. They thought the Americans would not hit them because it was between civilians," said Dr. Muhammad Hassan al-`Ubaidi of al-Najaf Teaching Hospital.

Coalition troops made similar allegations. Asked if he thought Iraqis sometimes used the location of military hardware to shield themselves, Colonel Lyle Cayce, staff judge advocate for the Third Infantry Division, "I don't think there is any question. Look at the entire pattern across the battlefield. Why put airplanes next to mosques? You can't fly from there."[217] Colonel Baldwin had the same impression after his experiences in southern Iraq. "It must have become clear infrastructure areas were avoided [by Coalition forces]. It wouldn't take the brains of an archbishop to figure it out," he said.[218] Baldwin described seeing a rocket launcher hidden in a village near Basra. "It

---

[217] Human Rights Watch telephone interview with Colonel Lyle Cayce. Colonel Cayce served as the division's lead attorney during the war and is now a student at the Army War College.

[218] Human Rights Watch telephone interview with Colonel Gil Baldwin.

could easily have been dug in in the desert," he said, noting there was "no tactical value" to its placement in the village.[219]

Asked about the causes of civilian casualties in Baghdad, Dr. `Ali al-Aharkhi, chief of neurosurgery at the Adnan Khiralla Hospital, said, "The real problem was weapons put by our government in between civilian areas. If you put tanks near houses, they will definitely be attacked. There was a tank in front of my house. [The military forces] refused to move it."[220]

Human Rights Watch also found examples of Iraqi troops failing to take any steps to protect the population, including the implementation of evacuation plans. Four residents in Nadir, for example, said no precautions had been taken to ensure their safety.[221] Residents of Hay al-Khadra'a in Baghdad provided similar testimony.[222] "There were . . . vehicles, armor, and weapons (anti-aircraft and rocket launchers) in the streets, highway, and homes. . . . The Iraqi forces did not make any attempt to evacuate us. They did nothing else to protect us and other civilians from the battle," said Munkith Fathi `Abd al-Razzaq.[223] On the contrary, it appears the Iraqi troops hoped the presence of civilians would deter enemy attacks.

The location of military objectives in civilian areas raises concerns under international humanitarian law. While IHL does not prohibit fighting in urban areas, it does require parties to an armed conflict to take precautions to protect civilians from the dangers of military operations.[224] If properly implemented these precautions should provide civilians some protection in situations of urban warfare. With regard to precautions taken against the effects of attacks, IHL requires parties to an armed conflict, "to the maximum extent feasible," to "avoid locating military objectives within or near densely

---

[219] Ibid.

[220] Human Rights Watch interview with Dr. `Ali al-Aharkhi, chief of neurosurgery, Adnan Khiralla Hospital, Baghdad, May 17, 2003.

[221] Human Rights Watch interview with Talib Madhlum `Abdullah; Human Rights Watch interview with Ahmad Khalaf Jabbar; Human Rights Watch interview with `Adil Sa`ad al-Shami; Human Rights Watch interview with `Ali Hassan Fakhr.

[222] Human Rights Watch interview with Munkith Fathi `Abd al-Razzaq; Human Rights Watch interview with Haidar Majed Suhail and Hazza` Majed Suhail; Human Rights Watch interview with Muhammad Salih Mahdi.

[223] Human Rights Watch interview with Munkith Fathi `Abd al-Razzaq.

[224] Protocol I, art. 57.

populated areas."[225] They should also "endeavor to remove the civilian population . . . from the vicinity of military objectives."[226]

While military targets such as combatants and military hardware and vehicles may end up in civilian areas during combat, it appears based on Human Rights Watch's observations that the Iraqi armed forces intentionally located military objectives in civilian areas well ahead of any combat operations. Human Rights Watch believes this practice, coupled with the failure to remove the civilian population from areas exposed to the dangers of fighting, amounts to a failure to take the precautions required by IHL against the effects of attacks.

Combatants in Civilian Clothes

Iraqi civilians around the country reported seeing Iraqi troops out of uniform. Dr. `Abd al-Sayyid, director of al-Nasiriyya General Hospital, blamed many of the civilian deaths in the battle of al-Nasiriyya on the practice. "Fedayeen were among the civilian homes. . . . [T]he problem was with the Iraqi troops and fedayeen dressed as civilians," he said.[227] Yusif Sahib Jawad, the taxi driver who lived along the main battle route in al-Najaf, said he saw Ba`thist and fedayeen combatants wearing civilian clothes.[228] Qassim Abu Ahmad, 35, witnessed the battle in al-Yarmuk neighborhood of Baghdad. He reported that all of the fedayeen he saw in the street or on rooftops were dressed like civilians.[229] When asked how they knew these combatants were not civilians bearing arms, Iraqis generally replied that "everyone in the neighborhood knows" who is a civilian and who belongs to the army, Ba`th party militia, or fedayeen.[230]

Almost every member of the Coalition interviewed by Human Rights Watch commented on this practice. "By March 24 [the fourth day of the war], we were already seeing a large number of irregulars out of uniform. It was clearly a combination of systematic and conscious," said Colonel Baldwin, whose troops advanced up al-Fao Peninsula to

---

[225] Ibid., art. 58(b).

[226] Ibid., art. 58(a).

[227] Human Rights Watch interview with Dr. `Ali `Abd al-Sayyid, director, al-Nasiriyya General Hospital, al-Nasiriyya, May 7, 2003.

[228] Human Rights Watch interview with Yusif Sahib Jawad.

[229] Human Rights Watch interview with Qassim Abu Ahmad, Baghdad, May 22, 2003.

[230] See, e.g., Human Rights Watch telephone interview with `Abd al-Razzaq al-Sa`di, Baghdad, October 14, 2003.

Basra.[231] Major Samarov said the Marines encountered uniformed troops in the south, near Safwan, al-Zubayr, and Basra. "After that I'd be hard-pressed to think of any enemy not in civilian clothes," he said.[232] Other reports of Iraqi combatants fighting in civilian clothes came from Marines caught in an ambush along the route from al-Nasiriyya to al-Kut and the soldiers in the Second Brigade, Third Infantry Division, who fought in al-Najaf. [233] The Iraqis often combined such conduct with use of civilian vehicles, particularly orange-and-white taxis. On April 7, for example, Special Republican Guard forces launched a counterattack on Second Brigade forces entering Baghdad while firing from civilian vehicles and wearing civilian clothes.[234]

Such actions tend to erode the distinction between combatants and civilians and put the latter at risk. They do not, however, relieve the opposing side of its obligation to distinguish at all times between combatants and civilians and to target only combatants.[235] In case of doubt, a person must be considered a civilian.[236]

Conclusion and Recommendations

Iraqi forces committed a number of violations of international humanitarian law, which may have led to significant civilian casualties. These violations included use of human shields, abuse of the red cross and red crescent emblems, use of antipersonnel landmines, placement of military objects in protected places (such as mosques, hospitals, and cultural property sites), and failure to take adequate precautions to protect civilians from the dangers resulting from military operations. The Iraq military's practice of wearing civilian clothes tended to erode the distinction between combatants and civilians and put the latter at risk.

To prevent future IHL violations by Iraqi armed forces, Human Rights Watch recommends that the new Iraqi army be adequately trained in international humanitarian law and human rights law.

---

[231] Human Rights Watch telephone interview with Colonel Gil Baldwin.

[232] Human Rights Watch interview with Major Michael Samarov.

[233] Human Rights Watch interview with U.S. Marine officer #1, al-Hilla, May 20, 2003; Human Rights Watch interview with Colonel David Perkins.

[234] Human Rights Watch interview with Colonel David Perkins.

[235] Protocol I, art. 48.

[236] Ibid., art. 50(1).

Coalition Conduct in the Ground War

The Coalition took many precautions to spare civilians from the effects of the ground war, including vetting cluster munition strikes and giving guidance to troops involved in direct combat. The use by U.S. and U.K. ground forces of cluster munitions, especially in or near populated areas, however, was one of the major causes of civilian casualties in the war. Moreover, in some instances of direct combat, problems with training on as well as dissemination and clarity of the rules of engagement may have contributed to loss of civilian life.

Ground-Launched Cluster Munitions

The U.S. and U.K. use of ground-launched cluster munitions represented one of the major threats to civilians during the war. Unlike Coalition air forces, American and British ground forces used cluster munitions extensively in populated areas. Human Rights Watch found evidence of ground-launched submunitions (known as grenades) in residential neighborhoods across the country, including in Basra, al-Hilla, Karbala', al-Najaf, and Baghdad. A military list of duds reported after the war shows that the use of these weapons was widespread along the battle route to Baghdad, including in and around other populated areas.[237] While these strikes were directed at Iraqi military targets, the weapons' inaccuracy, broad footprints, and large numbers of submunitions caused hundreds of civilian casualties.

Use of Cluster Munitions

Coalition use of ground-launched cluster munitions far outstripped the use of air-dropped models. CENTCOM reported in October that it used a total of 10,782 cluster munitions,[238] which could contain between 1.7 and 2 million submunitions.[239]

---

[237] Humanitarian Operations Center, "Mine Data through 18 May 2003," obtained by Human Rights Watch, Kuwait City, Kuwait, June 1, 2003 [hereinafter HOC list, May 18, 2003]. Human Rights Watch obtained this list of mines, unexploded ordnance, and submunition duds, as well as two earlier versions, from representatives of the Army Corps of Engineers at the HOC. This list includes GPS coordinates where these kinds of explosive remnants of war were found.

[238] U.S. CENTCOM, executive summary of report on cluster munitions.

[239] The U.S. Air Force used 1,206 reported cluster bombs and an unknown number of TLAMs and JSOWs with submunitions. Human Rights Watch found little evidence of the latter two types, which suggests the vast majority of the 10,782 cluster munitions were ground-launched. If one subtracts the 1,206 reported cluster bombs and the 1,555 reported ground-launched munitions (discussed later in this paragraph) from CENTCOM's total, there are 8,021 unidentified cluster munitions. Given that ground forces used 17,423 artillery rounds, a large portion of those unidentified cluster munitions were probably artillery models, which contain seventy-two or eighty-eight submunitions. Taking the number of submunitions from identified cluster models and estimating the rest as if they were artillery models brings the estimated total of submunitions to between 1.7 and 2 million.

An Iraqi woman holds a U.S. submunition dud she found on her home in Nadir, a neighborhood of al-Hilla. The explosive had come out of the ground-launched DPICM shell so she was in no danger. Thirty-eight civilians were killed and 156 were injured in Nadir during and after the U.S. attack on March 31, 2003. © 2003 Marc Garlasco / Human Rights Watch

Although it did not break them down by type, field research and U.S. Air Force numbers suggest that the vast majority were ground-launched. Human Rights Watch found evidence of at least four types of artillery-, rocket-, and missile-delivered submunitions. The Third Infantry and 101st Airborne divisions and the 214th Field Artillery Brigade reported using 1,014 MLRS rockets, 330 Army Tactical Missile System (ATACMS) missiles, and 121 artillery shells with Sense and Destroy Armor Munitions (SADARMs), which carry at least 928,000 submunitions of varying types.[240] They also used 17,423 artillery rounds, an unknown number of which carried submunitions.[241] The United Kingdom, more forthcoming about its weapons choice, reported it used 2,100 ground-launched cluster munitions.[242] Its L20A1 artillery projectile contains forty-nine grenades, for a total of 102,900 submunitions, more than ten times the number of cluster bomblets the Royal Air Force dropped.

While information from CENTCOM and individual ground units has trickled in, the U.S. Army and Marine Corps have not released final numbers of cluster munitions they launched. Human Rights Watch called for more transparency on cluster use in an April 29 press release.[243] Five months after the war, a senior CENTCOM official said the information was still unavailable. "The process is continuing. Units on the battlefield are still on the battlefield, and I can't swear to the precision of record keeping. The guidance from CENTCOM and the Army and Marine Corps is to recreate to the best degree possible where munitions were used so we can provide back to the U.N. . . . a best guess of where they are [to facilitate clearance of duds]," the official said.[244] CENTCOM's release in October of a figure for total cluster munitions implies it has completed its counting process. Nevertheless, a complete breakdown by service branch and type of munition has yet to be made public.

U.S. and U.K. forces used these weapons to respond to or prevent incoming fire from Iraqi forces. U.S. ground forces deployed cluster munitions primarily as a counter-

---

[240] "Infantry Conference Summary," Infantry Online: Timely News for the Infantry Community, October 1, 2003, http://www.benning.army.mil/OLP/InfantryOnline/issue_39/art_255.htm (retrieved October 23, 2003); Rhett A. Taylor et al., "MLRS AFATDS and Communications," *Field Artillery*, July 1, 2003, p. 36. ATACMSs can carry 950 or 300 submunitions as will be discussed below. If the unidentified ATACMSs all contained 950 submunitions, the total would be 1,142,858.

[241] "Infantry Conference Summary." The M483 artillery projectile carries eighty-eight submunitions and the M864 artillery projectile carries seventy-two submunitions.

[242] Ann Treneman, "Mapped: The Lethal Legacy of Cluster Bombs," *Times* (London), September 11, 2003.

[243] Human Rights Watch, "Iraq: Clusters Info Needed from U.S., U.K.," Press Release, April 29, 2003.

[244] Human Rights Watch telephone interview with senior CENTCOM official #2.

battery tool, i.e. to destroy enemy mortars and artillery and to kill the troops operating them. While six rounds of high explosive artillery, a unitary weapon that sends fragments fifty yards (forty-six meters) in every direction, was the "normal response" to incoming mortar fire, MLRS cluster munitions were used for longer-range targets.[245] Ground-launched clusters were also used for suppression of enemy air defense (SEAD) missions.[246] These missions sought to clear a safe path for Apache helicopters by attacking "man portable air defense," such as an Iraqi soldier with a shoulder-launched missile. They blanketed the path of a helicopter with submunitions, targeting places where such defense might have existed even if there was no observation to confirm it.[247] British ground forces used cluster munitions for their anti-armor and area effects. "If there's a twenty-tank convoy, if you use a precision-guided munition, you get one at a time. If you use a cluster munition, you get twenty in one hit," said Colonel Baldwin. For non-armored targets, the British fired high explosive artillery rounds.[248]

The majority of the U.S. submunitions used were Dual-Purpose Improved Conventional Munitions (DPICMs). Smaller than the air-dropped BLU-97, each DPICM grenade is 2.25 inches (5.5 centimeters) tall and 1.5 inch (3.5 centimeter) in diameter. Sometimes likened to a battery, it is a cylinder, usually gray, that has one hollow end and, at the other, a white ribbon that arms and stabilizes it during flight. It consists of a scored, steel fragmentation case with an armor-piercing shaped charge inside. The DPICM can be launched by artillery or rocket. A 155mm artillery projectile contains either eighty-eight or seventy-two M42 and M46 DPICMs, depending on the model.[249] The MLRS has twelve rockets, each with 644 M77 DPICMs. In Iraq, the standard volley of six rockets would release 3,864 submunitions over an area with a .6-mile (one-kilometer) radius.[250] Both delivery systems leave shockingly large quantities of duds; the artillery

---

[245] Human Rights Watch interview with Major Jim Barren, Second Brigade, Third Infantry Division, U.S. Army, Baghdad, May 23, 2003.

[246] Rhett A. Taylor et al., "MLRS AFATDS and Communications."

[247] See 101st Airborne (Air Assault), "Gold Book: Targets, Techniques, and Procedures for Air Assault Operations," March 17, 1999, annex F, http://www.fas.org/man/dod-101/army/docs/101st-goldbook/index.html (retrieved October 20, 2003).

[248] Human Rights Watch telephone interview with Colonel Gil Baldwin.

[249] The M483A1 contains sixty-four M42 and twenty-four M46 DPICM submunitions. The M864 contains forty-eight M42 and twenty-four M46 submunitions. For more information, see Human Rights Watch, "Cluster Munitions a Foreseeable Hazard in Iraq."

[250] The Third Infantry Division often used volleys of six rockets in Iraq. The footprints overlapped to make a larger footprint with .6-mile radius (one kilometer). Human Rights Watch telephone interview with Colonel Lyle Cayce.

projectiles have a dud rate of 14 percent, the MLRS a dud rate of 16 percent, about triple the Air Force estimate for BLU-97 bomblets.[251]

U.S. ground forces also used missile- and helicopter-launched submunitions. The ATACMS consists of a thirteen-foot-long (four-meter-long) missile fired from a modified MLRS. It contains 950 or 300 M74 softball-sized submunitions, each of which dispenses 195 fragments that target thin-skinned vehicles and personnel.[252] The reported dud rate is 2 percent.[253] The Hydra M261 rocket is launched from Apache or Cobra helicopters and contains nine submunitions with clover-leafed parachutes.[254] These M73 grenades have a reported 4 percent dud rate.[255]

For the first time in combat, the United States used the SADARM, a guided artillery-launched submunition.[256] Each 155mm shell contains two submunitions that use wave and infrared sensors to detect armored vehicles. If they find a target, they fire a penetrating slug that pierces armor. If they do not, they are designed to self-destruct.[257] Although further research will need be done to determine the weapon's humanitarian effects, a Third Infantry Division presentation on lessons learned in Iraq described the

---

[251] For the dud rate of MLRS submunitions, see Office of the Under Secretary of Defense for Acquisition, Technology, and Logistics, "Unexploded Ordnance Report," n.d., table 2-3, p. 5, transmitted to Congress on February 29, 2000. For the dud rate of submunitions in 155mm artillery munitions, see U.S. Army Defense Ammunition Center, Technical Center for Explosives Safety, "Study of Ammunition Dud and Low Order Detonation Rates," July 2000, p. 9. See also Human Rights Watch, "Cluster Munitions a Foreseeable Hazard in Iraq." The U.S. Air Force estimates the dud rate of the BLU-97 to be 5 percent although deminers in Afghanistan estimated the dud rate in some areas as 22 percent. Human Rights Watch, "Fatally Flawed," p. 25.

[252] FAS Military Analysis Network, "M39 Army Tactical Missile System (Army TACMS)," May 13, 2003, http://www.fas.org/man/dod-101/sys/land/atacms.htm (retrieved October 23, 2003); ORDATA Online, "U.S. Grenade, Frag, M74," February 4, 2002, http://maic.jmu.edu/ordata/srdetaildesc.asp?ordid=1088 (retrieved October 23, 2003).

[253] Office of the Under Secretary of Defense for Acquisition, Technology, and Logistics, "Unexploded Ordnance Report," table 2-3, p. 5.

[254] FAS Military Analysis Network, "Hydra-70 Rocket System," May 5, 2000, http://www.fas.org/man/dod-101/sys/missile/hydra-70.htm (retrieved October 23, 2003); ORDATA Online, "U.S. Grenade, HEDP, M73," February 4, 2002, http://maic.jmu.edu/ordata/srdetaildesc.asp?ordid=1099 (retrieved October 20, 2003).

[255] Office of the Under Secretary of Defense for Acquisition, Technology, and Logistics, "Unexploded Ordnance Report," table 2-3, p. 5.

[256] "3rd Infantry Division Commander Live Briefing from Iraq," U.S. Department of Defense News Transcript, May 15, 2003.

[257] FAS Military Analysis Network, "XM898 SADARM (Sense and Destroy Armor)," September 12, 1998, http://www.fas.org/man/dod-101/sys/land/sadarm.htm (retrieved November 7, 2003).

SADARM as a "winner," saying it was accurate and "very effective" against tanks and other armor.[258]

British ground forces used the L20A1 artillery projectile. It contains forty-nine M85 submunitions, which the United Kingdom used for the first time in combat in Iraq. These Israeli-designed grenades resemble the DPICM in shape, color, and purpose. They also have a self-destruct mechanism, however, that is designed to reduce the dud rate to 2 percent.[259]

Civilian Harm

Ground-launched cluster strikes caused hundreds of civilian casualties across Iraq. Human Rights Watch documented cases in most of the major cities, including al-Hilla, al-Najaf, Karbala', Baghdad, and Basra. Doctors at local hospitals provided statistics that supported individual testimony of deaths and injuries. The majority of these casualties resulted from the heavy use of cluster munitions in populated areas where soldiers and civilians commingled. The targeting of residential neighborhoods with these area effect weapons represented one of the leading causes of civilian casualties in the war.

Al-Hilla endured the most suffering from the use of ground-launched cluster munitions. Dr. Sa`ad al-Falluji, director and chief surgeon of al-Hilla General Teaching Hospital, said 90 percent of the injuries his hospital treated during the war were from submunitions.[260] In the neighborhood of Nadir, a slum on the south side of the city, every household Human Rights Watch visited suffered personal injury or property damage during a March 31 cluster attack. On the day of the strike, the hospital treated

---

[258] Third Infantry Division, "Fires in the Close Fight: OIF [Operation Iraqi Freedom] Lessons Learned," n.d., http://sill-www.army.mil/Fa/Lessons_Learned/3d%20ID%20Lessons%20Learned.pdf (retrieved November 10, 2003). The Third Infantry Division also reported that "SADARM killed 48 pieces of equipment out of 121 SADARM rounds fired." "Third Infantry Division (Mechanized) After Action Report, Operation Iraqi Freedom," July 2003, p. 122, http://www.carson.army.mil/Moblas/NBC/3rdIDAARIraqJuly03.pdf (retrieved October 23, 2003).

[259] Thomas Frank, "Officials: Hundreds of Iraqis Killed by Faulty Grenades," *Newsday*, June 22, 2003 (citing the British Ministry of Defence). The hazardous dud rate, i.e. percentage of submunitions that do not explode on impact but could detonate later, is designed to be less than one percent. FAS Military Analysis Network, "M26 Multiple Launch Rocket System (MLRS)," December 23, 1999, http://www.fas.org/man/dod-101/sys/land/m26.htm (retrieved October 22, 2003).

[260] Human Rights Watch interview with Dr. Sa`ad al-Falluji, director and chief surgeon, al-Hilla General Teaching Hospital, al-Hilla, May 19, 2003.

al-Hilla: Cluster Strikes on Homes in Nadir
al-Hilla
Cluster Strikes (HRW Data)
Cluster Strikes (HRW Data)
0
50
100
200
Meters
N
Satellite Image: Space Imaging. Photographed December 23, 2002

109 injured civilians from that neighborhood, including thirty children.[261] According to local elders, the attack killed thirty-eight civilians and injured 156.[262] During a visit on May 19, Human Rights Watch found dozens of mud brick homes with pockmarked walls and holes in the roof from shrapnel. Male residents pointed to wounds on their legs and pulled up their shirts to reveal chest and abdominal wounds. In the house of Falaya Fadl Nasir, for example, the strike injured three people, his two children, Mahdi, 18, and Marwa, 10, as well as Imam Hassan `Abdullah. One grenade pierced the roof of his home, causing a fire inside.[263] Hamid Turki Hamid, 36, a dresser in the hospital, said his son and a friend were in the street when the attack began. After bringing in his son, he returned to gather his neighbor's child. "That's when the bomb exploded, when I was injured," Hamid said.[264]

Cluster munitions caused civilian casualties in other neighborhoods in and around al-Hilla. On March 31 at about 2:00 p.m., the U.S. Army launched DPICMs on al-Maimira, a village of about 500 people south of al-Hilla. The strike killed three civilians—Amir Ahmad, 9, Jawad Ruman, 27, and Khalid `Abbas, 32—and injured thirty-eight. A villager said there was no battle in the area and speculated that the strike was aimed at guns on the main road and across the river or civilian lorries mistaken for a military convoy.[265] During an attack on al-Mahawil at 1:00 p.m. around April 3, cluster grenades killed four civilians and injured five, most of whom had to have limbs amputated. One woman, who was nine months pregnant, had an amputation and an injury to her womb; the baby had shrapnel in it but survived.[266]

---

[261] Of the 109 civilians, twenty-eight were women (including eleven girls) and eighty-one were male (including nineteen boys). Al-Hilla General Teaching Hospital, War-Related Casualty Records, obtained by Human Rights Watch, al-Hilla, May 20, 2003.

[262] The neighborhood elders did not separate casualties that occurred during the strike from those caused by duds after the fact. Their casualty records list 144 men, 37 women, and 17 whose sex could not be determined. Shakir `Abadi `Ubaid al-Khafaji, Kadhim Karim `Ali al-Jaburi, and Hassan Jum`a Sayyid, Nadir Casualty Records, obtained by Human Rights Watch, al-Hilla, September 2003. The *New York Times* said thirty-three civilians died during the strike on Nadir. Tyler Hicks and John F. Burns, "Iraq Shows Casualties in Hospital," *New York Times*, April 3, 2003.

[263] Human Rights Watch interview with Falaya Fadl Nasir, al-Hilla, May 19, 2003.

[264] Human Rights Watch interview with Hamid Turki Hamid, al-Hilla, May 19, 2003.

[265] Human Rights Watch interview with Tahsin `Ali, al-Maimira, May 20, 2003.

[266] Human Rights Watch interview with Khalil Nahi Athab, al-Hilla, May 20, 2003.

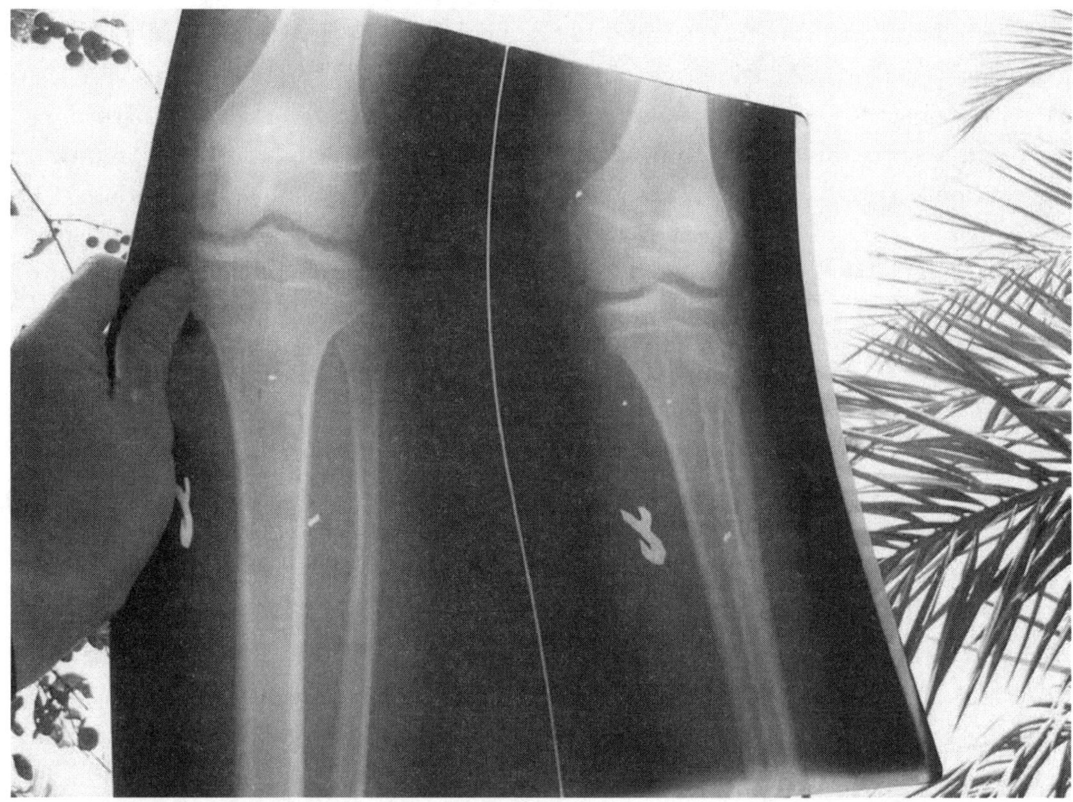

Dr. Sa`ad al-Falluji inspects the X-ray of a patient with shrapnel still lodged in his leg in al-Maimira, outside al-Hilla. Three civilians were killed and thirty-eight injured during a U.S. ground-launched cluster strike on the village. © 2003 Marc Garlasco / Human Rights Watch

The harm to civilians caused by ground-launched submunitions in al-Hilla exemplified a pattern seen around the country. In al-Najaf, cluster grenades killed about thirty-six civilians on the night of March 28 alone.[267] "The day of the bombing was a horrible day. There were not enough places to keep the dead people. Many of the dead people were in the lobbies of the hospital. . . . Later families came and took them. The government buried unknown people in the cemeteries," said Dr. Safa' al-`Umaidi, director of al-Najaf Teaching Hospital.[268] The nearby al-Najaf General Hospital treated fewer patients during the war, but the director said most of the injuries he saw came from cluster munitions.[269] A cluster strike that landed in Hay al-Karama at 1:00 a.m. on March 27 caused many civilian casualties. Hatim Jawad, a 52-year-old merchant, for

---

[267] Human Rights Watch interview with Dr. Safa' al-`Umaidi, director, al-Najaf Teaching Hospital, al-Najaf, May 24, 2003.

[268] Ibid.

[269] Human Rights Watch interview with Dr. `Ali al-Tufaili. Dr. al-Tufaili added, however, "The military of Saddam was in between our homes. Therefore the best way to deal with them was with clusters. . . . If not for clusters, the injured would have been more."

example, suffered shrapnel wounds as well as severe damage to his home.[270] Another man approached Human Rights Watch crying and clutching a piece of bone he said was part of his late sister's skull.[271]

The villages around al-Najaf also suffered casualties from ground cluster strikes. At sunset on March 28, cluster grenades landed on the farm of Jassim `Abdul-Ridha, 31, in al-Hifa, southeast of al-Najaf. Two months later, his 10-year-old son, Nussair, who had been tending sheep during the strike, was still in the hospital recovering from skin grafts, fractures, and bone loss in his ankle. His other son, Muhammad Jassim, 7, had been injured at the same time but had returned home. Two neighbor children were hurt in this strike: Jassim Muhammad, 6, suffered paralysis and received additional shrapnel wounds in his abdomen and upper leg; his brother Ja`far Muhammad, 3, suffered head injuries that led to apparent brain damage.[272] At a different farm west of al-Najaf, three brothers were sitting in their garden when a strike occurred around March 22.[273] Salim Hashim, 26, lost his left hand and suffered injuries to his chest, leg, right thigh, shoulder, and face; he remained in the hospital on May 24. Hamid Hashim, 23, received shrapnel injuries to his head and eye, and Hani Hashim, 20, was injured in his hand.[274]

U.S. ground forces also made extensive use of cluster munitions in and around Baghdad. At 2:00 a.m. on the night of April 4 to 5, DPICMs rained down on an apartment complex next to a Palestinian refugee camp in northeast Baghdad.[275] The submunitions killed at least one civilian, Radwan Muhammad, and injured about eighteen others.[276] "When they started bombing the area, I was standing with four persons. All were injured. The explosion hit my eyes and I couldn't see because of the big light," said Ahmad Yahir Ahmad Salama al-Hadidi, 45.[277] He still has shrapnel in his body and has

---

[270] Human Rights Watch interview with Hatim Jawad, al-Najaf, May 24, 2003.

[271] Human Rights Watch interview with resident of Hay al-Karama, al-Najaf, May 24, 2003.

[272] Human Rights Watch interview with Jassim `Abdul-Ridha, al-Najaf, May 24, 2003. `Abdul-Ridha, a 31-year-old farmer, is the father of Nussair and Muhammad. Medical information was provided by Dr. Muhammad Hassan al-`Ubaidi. Human Rights Watch interview with Dr. Muhammad Hassan al-`Ubaidi, doctor, al-Najaf Teaching Hospital, and assistant professor, College of Medicine, University of Kufa, al-Najaf, May 24, 2003.

[273] Since this strike occurred before the main battle in al-Najaf, it could have been a SEAD mission.

[274] Human Rights Watch interview with Salim Hashim, al-Najaf, May 24, 2003; Human Rights Watch interview with Dr. Muhammad Hassan al-`Ubaidi.

[275] Human Rights Watch interview with Ahmad Yahir Ahmad Salama al-Hadidi, Baghdad, May 16, 2003.

[276] Human Rights Watch interview with Anwar Salim al-`Awawda, director, Palestine Clinic, Baghdad, May 16, 2003.

[277] Human Rights Watch interview with Ahmad Yahir Ahmad Salama al-Hadidi, Baghdad, May 16, 2003.

difficulty breathing because of burn damage to his lungs.[278] Residents speculated that the strike targeted Syrian fedayeen outside their homes or an anti-aircraft position at a nearby intersection. This strike was one of many in the capital area.[279] A list of submunition duds from the U.S. military, which provides an indication of where strikes occurred, includes 166 sites within a twenty-kilometer (12.4-mile) radius of Baghdad.[280]

U.K. forces caused dozens of civilian casualties when they used ground-launched cluster munitions in and around Basra. A trio of neighborhoods in the southern part of the city was particularly hard hit. At noon on March 23, a cluster strike hit Hay al-Muhandissin al-Kubra (the engineers' district) while `Abbas Kadhim, 13, was throwing out the garbage. He had acute injuries to his bowel and liver, and a fragment that could not be removed lodged near his heart. On May 4, he was still in Basra's al-Jumhuriyya Hospital.[281] Three hours later, submunitions blanketed the neighborhood of al-Mishraq al-Jadid about two-and-a-half kilometers (one-and-a-half miles) northeast. Iyad Jassim Ibrahim, a 26-year-old carpenter, was sleeping in the front room of his home when shrapnel injuries caused him to lose consciousness. He later died in surgery. Ten relatives who were sleeping elsewhere in the house suffered shrapnel injuries.[282] Across the street, the cluster strike injured three children. Ahmad `Aidan Malih Hoshon, 12, and his sister Fatima, 4, both had serious abdominal injuries; their cousin Muhammad, 13, had injuries to his feet.[283] Hay al-Zaitun, just east of al-Mishraq al-Jadid, suffered casualties from cluster munitions that landed there on the evening of March 25. Jamal

---

[278] Ibid.

[279] The press reported several cluster strikes in Baghdad. See, e.g., Carol Rosenberg and Matt Schofield, "In Bombed Neighborhoods, Everyone 'Wants to Kill Americans,'" Miami Herald.com, April 15, 2003, http://www.miami.com/mld/miamiherald/5640621.htm (retrieved October 24, 2003) (cluster duds killed four civilians in al-Kharnouq neighborhood); "Iraq Says U.S. Drops Cluster Bombs on Baghdad, 14 Die," Reuters, April 3, 2003 (cluster bombs kill fourteen civilians and wound sixty-six in al-Dura neighborhood); Thomas Frank, "Grisly Results of U.S. Cluster Bombs," *Newsday*, April 15, 2003 (the Kadhimiya Hospital treated cluster victims from several Baghdad neighborhoods); Jonathan Steele, "Iraq—after the War—Bombs Silent, but the Children Still Suffer," *Guardian*, April 18, 2003 (cluster bombs caused civilian casualties in the Harir city neighborhood and areas around the Kadhimiya Hospital); Rosalind Russell, "Cluster Bombs: A Hidden Enemy for Iraqi Children," Reuters, April 18, 2003 (cluster duds injure children in al-Dura district); "Iraqi Children Facing Threat of Bomblets Left Over by U.S. Forces," Xinhua News Agency, April 19, 2003 (cluster duds injure civilians in Rahnania in western Baghdad and in al-Dura in southeastern Baghdad).

[280] See HOC list, May 18, 2003.

[281] Human Rights Watch interview with `Abbas Kadhim, Basra, May 4, 2003.

[282] The injured were Iyad Jassim Ibrahim, born 1970, fireman; `Imad Jassim Ibrahim, born 1971, laborer; Fu'ad Jassim Ibrahim, born 1974; Ibtisam Jassim Ibrahim, born 1975; Jihan Hassan Ahmad, born 1975, wife of Fu'ad; Lika Fadl Nasr, born 1982, wife of `Imad; Lou'ay `Imad Jassim, 4 years old, son of `Imad; Zakia Hussain Aziz, born 1946, mother of `Imad; Manal Jassim Ibrahim, born 1980, sister of `Imad; and `Athra Taha Jassim, born 1973, brother of `Imad. Human Rights Watch interview with Iyad Jassim Ibrahim, Basra, May 5, 2003.

[283] Human Rights Watch interview with Ahmad `Aidan Malih Hoshon, Basra, May 5, 2003.

Kamil Sabir, a 25-year-old laborer, lost his leg to a submunition blast while crossing a bridge near his home with his family. He spent eleven days in the hospital. His nephew, Jabal Kamil, 22, took shrapnel in his knee. Jamal's pregnant wife, Zainab Nasir `Abbas, still had shrapnel in her left leg in May because doctors were afraid to remove it during her pregnancy.[284] A neighbor, Zaitun Zaki Abu Iyad, 40, was killed when cluster grenades landed on her home.[285]

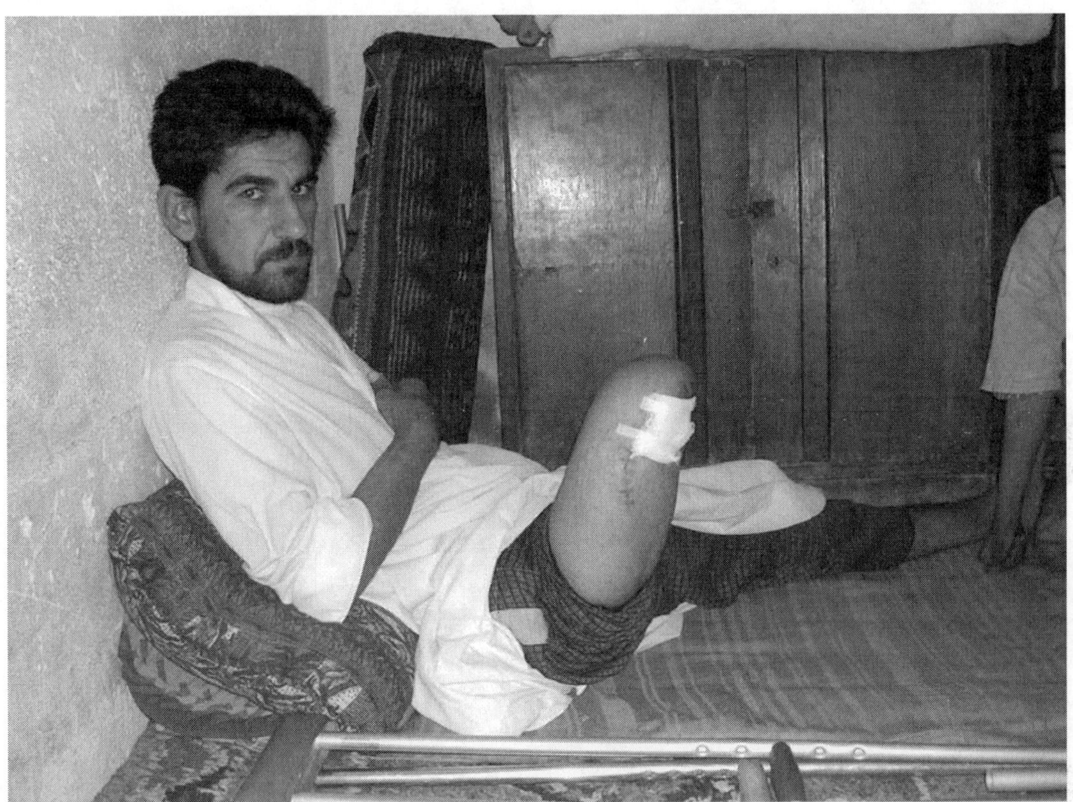

Jamal Kamil Sabir lost his right leg during a U.K. cluster munition strike on his home in Hay al-Zaitun in Basra on March 25, 2003. © 2003 Reuben E. Brigety, II / Human Rights Watch

Human Rights Watch also found evidence of ground-launched submunitions in other areas of Basra. In al-Tannuma neighborhood, on the eastern bank of Shatt al-`Arab, U.K. artillery targeted Iraqi tanks hidden in a date grove in the middle of civilian homes. The cluster grenades blanketed a much larger area. When the strike occurred on March 30 at 4:45 a.m., nine members of Tha'ir Zaidan's family were injured. Shrapnel lodged in

---

[284] Human Rights Watch interview with Jamal Kamil Sabir, Basra, May 1, 2003.

[285] Human Rights Watch interview with Hassan `Ali `Abud, Basra, May 2, 2003. `Abud, a 27-year-old laborer, was the victim's nephew. Other victims included Sabah Hamid, a 30-year-old laborer, and Hashim Hussain Muhammad, a 28-year-old laborer, who were both injured. Human Rights Watch interview with Hashim Hussain Muhammad, Basra, May 1, 2003.

the head of his young son, Hassan.[286] On the opposite side of the city, cluster munitions targeted Iraqi troops in al-Hadi neighborhood. The strike killed Sa`ad Sha`ban, 40, and Bassam Ghali, 35.[287]

It appears that most if not all of the strikes described above were directed at legitimate military targets. Human Rights Watch saw tanks and artillery positions located in neighborhoods, and witnesses described the presence of Iraqi forces. Nevertheless, the United States and United Kingdom made poor weapons choices when they used cluster munitions in populated areas. Such strikes almost always caused civilian casualties, in the case of al-Hilla numbering more than one hundred, because the weapons blanketed areas occupied by soldier and civilian alike with deadly submunitions that could not distinguish between the two.

Targeting and Technology

Both the U.S. and U.K. militaries took precautions to limit civilian casualties by establishing a process for vetting ground-launched cluster strikes. As shown above, however, such attacks were one of the major causes of civilian casualties during the war. The precautions failed for two reasons. First, the technology available to Coalition ground forces, in terms of range, accuracy, and reliability of cluster munitions, fell far behind that of the U.S. Air Force. Second, despite the vetting process, ground troops consistently used these area effect weapons in residential neighborhoods, virtually guaranteeing loss of civilian life. Coalition militaries should reevaluate and reform their use of ground-delivered cluster munitions before employing them in any future conflict.

U.S. forces screened ground cluster strikes through a computer and human vetting system. The Third Infantry Division's artillery batteries were programmed with a no-strike list of 12,700 sites that could not be fired upon without manual override. The list included civilian buildings such as schools, mosques, hospitals, and historic sites.[288]

---

[286] Human Rights Watch interview with Tha'ir Zaidan, Basra, May 30, 2003.

[287] Human Rights Watch interview with Hussain Sa`dan, Basra, May 30, 2003.

[288] Human Rights Watch interview with Lieutenant Colonel Eric Wesley, executive officer, Second Brigade, Third Infantry Division, U.S. Army, Baghdad, May 23, 2003.

Basra: U.K. Cluster Munition Strikes on Hay al-Zaitun

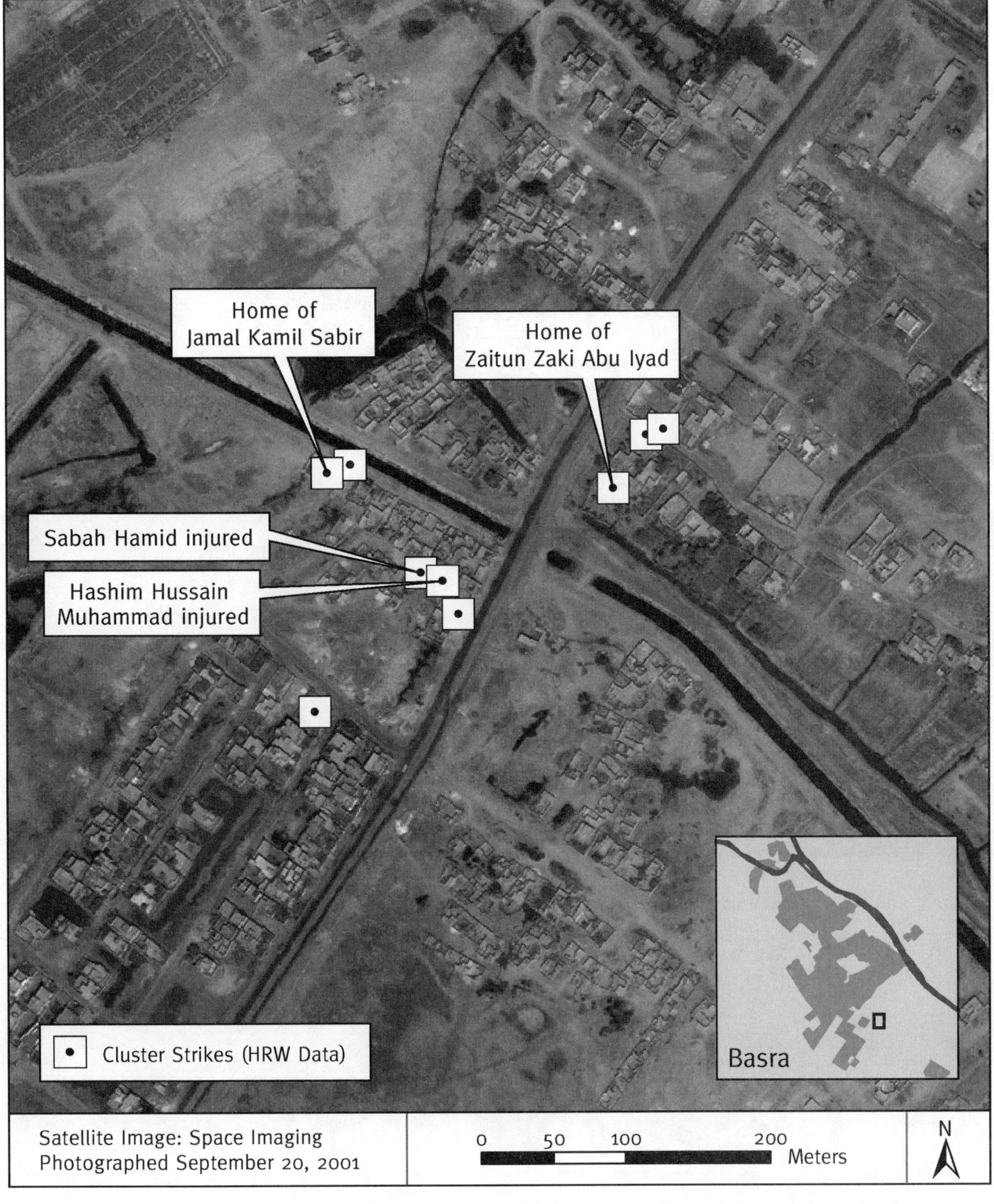

Officers of the Second Brigade said they strove to keep strikes at least 500 meters (547 yards) away from such targets although sometimes they cut the buffer zone to 300 meters (328 yards).[289] In general, they also required visual confirmation of a target before firing, but in the case of counter-battery fire, they considered radar acquisition sufficient.[290] The latter detects incoming fire and determines its location, but it cannot determine if civilians occupy an area.

The Third Infantry Division established another layer of review by sending lawyers to the field to review proposed strikes, a relatively recent addition to the vetting process.[291] "Ten years ago, JAGs [judge advocate general attorneys] weren't running around [the battlefield]," said Captain Chet Gregg, Second Brigade's legal advisor.[292] The division assigned sixteen lawyers to divisional headquarters and each brigade.[293] Lead lawyer Colonel Cayce, who served at the tactical headquarters, reviewed 512 missions, and brigade JAGs approved additional attacks, which were often counter-battery strikes. Although less controversial strikes, such as those on forces in the desert, were not reviewed, Cayce said, "I would feel pretty confident a lawyer was involved in strikes in populated areas."[294] Commanders had the final say, but lawyers provided advice about whether a strike was legal under IHL. Cayce said his commander never overruled his advice not to attack and sometimes rejected targets he said were legal.[295]

While the review process involved a careful weighing of military necessity and potential harm to civilians, limited information and the subjectivity of such an analysis meant it was "not a scientific formula."[296] The first challenge was to determine the risk to their forces. "The hard part is how many casualties we will take. It's a gut level, fly by the seat of your pants. There's no standard that says one U.S. life equals X civilian lives,"

---

[289] Ibid.

[290] Ibid. Although not specifically discussing ground-launched cluster strikes, a military conference about the lessons learned in the war said the Third Infantry Division needed to expand human intelligence capability and have unmanned aerial vehicles (UAVs), or drones, at a divisional and brigade combat team level. "Infantry Conference Summary."

[291] Human Rights Watch interview with Colonel David Perkins.

[292] Human Rights Watch interview with Captain Chet Gregg, legal advisor, Second Brigade, Third Infantry Division, U.S. Army, Baghdad, May 23, 2003.

[293] Human Rights Watch telephone interview with Colonel Lyle Cayce.

[294] Ibid.

[295] Ibid.

[296] Ibid.

Cayce said.[297] Then lawyers had to evaluate the threat to civilians. In the case of counter-battery fire, they had to make the judgment without knowing if civilians were present in the target area at the time of the strike; they relied instead on pre-war population figures. Cayce acknowledged the danger of cluster strikes on populated areas and said that he tried to limit them to nighttime. "I was hoping kids were hunkered down, hoping with artillery fire they were not out watching," he said.[298]

British artillery units had a similar vetting process although it gave observers more responsibility than lawyers. Its no-strike list included schools, mosques, and hospitals. "We couldn't fire on [such a site] irrespective of who was in it. Even if you called for fire, it couldn't happen. They were no-fire zones," said Colonel Baldwin.[299] Unlike the U.S. forces, the British required forward observation even in the case of counter-battery fire. Either a human or the video of an unmanned aerial vehicle (UAV), or drone, had to confirm visually that no civilians were present. "At no time did we fire where we couldn't see," Baldwin said.[300] Asked about the civilian injuries in al-Tannuma, he said, "I cannot completely rule out the fact somebody went against the ROE, but I'd be surprised if they did. For every single artillery strike, we asked an observer if he saw civilians."[301]

While the British required observers, they did not have lawyers in the field. Military lawyers signed off on the rules of engagement before the conflict, but the interpretation was done at a divisional level, if there was time, or below that, if the conflict was happening too fast. "If [the battle was] so fast and furious, interpretation went down to the forward observer. We argue they are the best judge of if we should fire or not," Colonel Baldwin said.[302]

The value of these vetting processes for cluster strikes was limited by the weapons and technology available to ground troops. Officers of the Third Infantry Division complained that if they needed long-range rocket artillery, the MLRS with submunitions was the only option they had. Therefore, they said, they often had to use cluster

---

[297] Ibid.

[298] Human Rights Watch telephone interview with Colonel Lyle Cayce.

[299] Human Rights Watch telephone interview with Colonel Gil Baldwin.

[300] Ibid.

[301] Ibid.

[302] Ibid.

munitions for counter-battery fire when a unitary warhead would have sufficed.[303] "We need to have the capability to hit a target [with something] more like a regular high explosive shell. . . . We are already testing longer-range cannon with a regular shell. It would solve a lot of problems," Colonel Cayce said.[304] A high explosive shell impacts an area with a fifty-yard (forty-six-meter) radius rather than the .6-mile (one-kilometer) radius of an MLRS volley.[305] The U.S. Marines, however, did not have the MLRS, relying instead on artillery, air support, and possibly help from Army ATACMSs.[306] These alternatives raise questions about the military necessity of the Army's MLRS cluster strikes.

Ground-launched cluster munitions were also less accurate than the newer, air-dropped models. "In defense of the ground guys, I have to say we have not come the distance in ability to be precise with [ground-launched] cluster munitions to the degree we have with the air. . . . The Army is working on coming the extra mile on precision-guided munitions," a senior CENTCOM official said.[307] Colonel Cayce also called for more accurate long-range artillery. He said the Army was developing a guided skeet, like that in the CBU-105, for the MLRS.[308] The SADARM is guided, but it is artillery-launched and does not have a range equal to the MLRS. In the Third Infantry Division's after action report, it recommended the development of "an MLRS suite of munitions that allow for greater employment on the battlefield," including in populated areas.[309]

Unlike the Americans, the British ground forces used exclusively new cluster technology in Iraq—the L20A1 artillery munition. While this weapon's submunitions have a lower dud rate than the U.S. versions, it remains an area effect weapon that kills civilians when

---

[303] Human Rights Watch interview with Colonel David Perkins; Human Rights Watch interview with Lieutenant Colonel Eric Wesley; Human Rights Watch interview with Major Jim Barren.

[304] Human Rights Watch telephone interview with Colonel Lyle Cayce.

[305] Ibid.

[306] Ibid.

[307] Human Rights Watch telephone interview with senior CENTCOM official #2.

[308] Human Rights Watch telephone interview with Colonel Lyle Cayce.

[309] "The only munitions currently available for standard MLRS rockets are the DPICM sub-munition. The ROE limited our ability to use MLRS in many cases. Fires in highly congested areas and civilian populace centers precluded the use of MLRS fires, especially within the city confines of Baghdad. Development of different types of MLRS munitions such as SADARM, brilliant antiarmor submunitions (BAT), smoke type precision munitions, and an HE [high explosive] conventional rocket similar to the Unitary missile would have greatly added to the flexibility in employing MLRS," the report said. "Third Infantry Division (Mechanized) After Action Report, Operation Iraqi Freedom," p. 122. See also Rhett A. Taylor et al., "MLRS AFATDS and Communications" (calling for a GPS-guided high explosive rocket).

used in a populated area. The new technology only lulled the British into taking less care when using it.[310]

The precautions to reduce civilian casualties did not prevent widespread use of cluster munitions in populated areas. The no-strike lists included certain civilian structures but not residential neighborhoods. Forward observers either ignored or failed to see civilians in populated areas. U.S. military lawyers did not challenge the proposed strikes although they raise serious concerns under IHL's proportionality test.

Training may also have been inadequate. "The training paradigm for artillery is still evolving," a senior CENTCOM official said. "The Army looks for mass of fire as opposed to precision because they don't know what's out there beyond the horizon. As they press forward, they want to make sure they are reducing the threat to their forces, suppressing what's beyond the next horizon."[311] An Army field manual acknowledges the dangerous side effects of cluster munitions and discusses ways to limit the collateral damage of strikes in urban areas, but it does not prohibit them or consider them indiscriminate.[312]

The Coalition may have fired on legitimate military targets, especially when responding to incoming Iraqi fire, but the use of cluster munitions in populated areas almost always leads to civilian casualties. For that weapon, neighborhoods still occupied by their residents should be put on a no-strike list, to be overridden only with excellent information and careful consideration.

Conclusion and Recommendations

As described in more depth in the previous chapter, cluster munition strikes raise concerns under international humanitarian law. They must be evaluated on a case-by-case basis under the proportionality test, which balances military advantage and civilian

---

[310] Human Rights Watch telephone interview with Colonel Gil Baldwin. For further discussion, see the New Technology section of the Explosive Remnants of War chapter.

[311] Human Rights Watch telephone interview with senior CENTCOM official #2.

[312] The field manual says, "Commanders must still consider the precision error and large submunitions dispersion pattern when applying this method of attack due to the high probability of extensive collateral damage" and explains that MLRS rockets require "detailed planning in close operations." It also warns of using these weapons near friendly troops because of their duds. Department of the Army, Headquarters, "Tactics, Techniques, and Procedures for Multiple Launch Rocket System (MLRS) Operations," Field Manual 6-60, Washington, D.C., April 23, 1996. The U.S. Army does not go as far as the U.S. Air Force, however, which has said there are "[c]learly some areas where CBUs normally couldn't be used (e.g. populated city centers)." U.S. Air Force, Bullet Background Paper on International Legal Aspects Concerning the Use of Cluster Munitions.

impact. Strikes in or near populated areas are usually problematic because when combatants and civilians commingle, civilian casualties are difficult to avoid. Cluster munition strikes also have the potential to be indiscriminate because the weapons cannot be precisely targeted. Cluster munitions are area weapons, useful in part for attacking dispersed or moving targets. They cannot, however, be directed at specific soldiers or tanks, a limitation that is particularly troublesome in populated areas.

In choosing weapons, parties to an armed conflict must minimize civilian harm. They must "take all feasible precautions in the choice of means and methods of attack with a view to avoiding, and in any event to minimizing, incidental loss of civilian life, injury to civilians and damage to civilian objects."[313] The weapons should be used sparingly, if at all, when it is foreseeable that they will cause at least incidental harm to civilians. The availability of alternative weapons must be also considered.

The use of cluster munitions in the ground war raises serious questions under these provisions of IHL. The weapons themselves have inherent flaws that make strikes in populated areas prone to being indiscriminate. Furthermore, while the Coalition took precautions by establishing vetting processes for individual strikes, the results show them to be inadequate. Despite the care taken, ground-launched cluster strikes caused hundreds of civilian casualties. As will be discussed below, the duds they left behind increased the number of deaths and injuries after the conflict.

Human Rights Watch has previously called for a suspension of cluster munition use until the weapon's humanitarian effects have been fully addressed.[314] If cluster munitions are used, Human Rights Watch recommends:

- Armed forces cease using ground-launched cluster munitions in or near populated areas.

- Coalition forces develop a new vetting process that successfully reduces the harm to civilians caused by cluster munitions.

- The U.S. military identify, and if necessary develop, a long-range alternative to the MLRS with submunitions.

---

[313] Protocol I, art. 57(2)(a)(ii).

[314] Human Rights Watch, Cluster Bombs: Memorandum for Convention on Conventional Weapons (CCW) Delegates, December 16, 1999.

- U.S. ground forces keep better records of the number, location, and type of cluster munitions used. Such records are essential for clearance of duds and also facilitate analysis of and accountability for targeting decisions.

Antipersonnel Landmines

The United States refused to rule out use of antipersonnel mines in Iraq, saying on one occasion that American forces might use air-dropped mines to prevent access to suspected chemical weapons sites.[315] By February 2003, the United States reportedly had stockpiled ninety thousand antipersonnel mines in Bahrain, Kuwait, Oman, Qatar, and Saudi Arabia.[316] There have been no confirmed reports, however, of antipersonnel mine use by the United States or other Coalition forces during the conflict. The head of the Coalition Provisional Authority stated, "We have constructed no minefields, set no 'booby traps' anywhere in Iraq."[317] U.S. forces used command-detonated Claymore directional fragmentation mines, which are permitted under the 1997 Mine Ban Treaty.[318] Like Iraq, the United States is not a party to the Mine Ban Treaty, but most of its Coalition partners, including the United Kingdom and Australia, are. Human Rights Watch believes any use of antipersonnel mines violates customary international law.

Rules of Engagement

Although the United States took precautions to protect civilians by issuing rules of engagement, problems with training on, dissemination of, and clarity of these rules may have, in some instances, contributed to loss of civilian life.

The U.S. military provided guidelines for its troops by distributing laminated rules of engagement cards to all its soldiers and Marines. These ROE, issued by the CENTCOM's Combined Forces Land Component Commander (CFLCC), tell troops to obey the laws of war and explain their legal obligations during combat. The first provision states, "Positive identification (PID) is required prior to engagement. PID is a reasonable certainty that the proposed target is a legitimate military target. If no PID,

---

[315] U.S. Department of Defense, "Background Briefing on Targeting," March 5, 2003.

[316] Alexander G. Higgins, "Campaigners Fear Use of Land Mines in Iraq," Associated Press, February 6, 2003.

[317] Remarks by L. Paul Bremer, III, administrator, Coalition Provisional Authority, at the Mine Action Management Course Graduation, July 31, 2003,

http://cpa-iraq.org/pressconferences/mine_removal_ceremony31jul03.html (retrieved November 5, 2003).

[318] U.S. CENTCOM, "CENTCOM Operation Iraqi Freedom Briefing," March 31, 2003.

contact your next higher commander for decision." Other paragraphs set out additional protections for civilians. For example:

> Do not target or strike any of the following except in self-defense to protect yourself, your unit, friendly forces, and designated persons or property under your control:
>
> - Civilians
>
> - Hospitals, mosques, national monuments, and any other historical and cultural sites.
>
> Do not fire into civilian populated areas or buildings unless the enemy is using them for military purposes or if necessary for your self-defense. Minimize collateral damage.[319]

The ROE card, reprinted in full as an appendix to this report, is consistent with international humanitarian law. The armed forces develop general ROE for each armed conflict. Individual operations within each conflict may also have their own specific set of rules of engagement, tailored to the particular circumstances of the battle.

Soldiers and Marines interviewed by Human Rights Watch said they tried to abide by these rules. Colonel Perkins of the Third Infantry Division said when faced with fedayeen in civilian vehicles, his troops would use a spotter to let them know which cars were safe to target. "We tried to delineate between civilian and military targets. . . . On the fifth and on the seventh [of April] when we attacked [Baghdad] the majority of what you can hear is, 'OK, can you see the white vehicle? He just shot at our guys. He's an enemy. The blue guy behind him is friendly, don't engage him,'" Perkins said.[320]

Training on the application of rules of engagement, however, may have been insufficient. Elements of the Third Infantry Division practiced urban combat tactics "all the time" in Kuwait, but the training focused on teaching soldiers how to clear a room in close combat quarters, not how to engage an unconventional enemy whose forces may wear civilian clothes.[321] A military conference about lessons learned from the war

---

[319] CFLCC, "CFLCC ROE Card," January 31, 2003.

[320] Human Rights Watch interview with Colonel David Perkins.

[321] Human Rights Watch interview with Lieutenant Colonel Stephen Baer, operations officer, Third Infantry Division, U.S. Army, Baghdad, May 20, 2003; Human Rights Watch interview with Sergeant First Class Morales.

emphasized the need better to prepare troops for dealing with ROE. Its list of lessons includes "Rules of Engagement (ROE) vignette training is critical in ensuring soldiers in contemporary operational environment (COE) adhere to laws of land warfare."[322]

Post-conflict analysis by the Third Infantry Division indicates problems with dissemination of the rules of engagement. According to the division's after action report, the final ROE, which included "new guidance on high collateral-damage targets," arrived after its troops had moved to Kuwait. "Late receipt of ROE caused confusion on a number of issues that were not clearly written. These matters were not resolved until hostilities began, meaning we could not train soldiers on the provision," the report said.[323]

During the war, especially in the battles of Baghdad and al-Nasiriyya, contradictions in, lack of consistency in, and/or misapplication of rules of engagement may have led to civilian casualties. In particular, verbal ROE apparently differed from the official written ROE, most notably with respect to the requirement for positive identification prior to engagement.

From April 5 to 7, the Third Infantry Division pushed its way into Baghdad in an advance known as Thunder Run. Contradictions in verbal and written rules of engagement may have led to civilian casualties. Junior U.S. soldiers who participated in Thunder Run said that on April 7 the verbal ROE from their immediate superiors were to "assume that all targets were hostile" rather than to obtain positive identification. They said that the verbal ROE were changed on April 9 to allow them to engage targets only when they were fired upon.

Colonel Perkins, who led Thunder Run, said that ROE guidance for his troops was: "Don't take anything for granted; assume that people have the capability to kill you, but don't assume that everyone is hostile." He said hostile intent would be demonstrated if (1) a target fired at a soldier, (2) a target carried a weapon, or (3) a target was driving toward U.S. forces at a high rate of speed.[324] Division lawyer Colonel Cayce explained that after Iraqi combatants began to appear in civilian clothes, soldiers were warned that any civilian could be a potential combatant, but they still needed positive

---

[322] "Infantry Conference Summary." The Infantry Conference took place at Fort Benning, Georgia, from September 8 to 11, 2003, and included representatives from many of the U.S. infantry units that fought in Iraq.

[323] "Third Infantry Division (Mechanized) After Action Report, Operation Iraqi Freedom," p. 286.

[324] Human Rights Watch interview with Colonel David Perkins.

identification.[325] Asked about the discrepancy between his version and that of the enlisted men, Perkins suggested that some soldiers may have incorrectly interpreted the guidance they were given, but that such interpretations did not accurately reflect the commander's intent or explicit text of the ROE promulgated by CFLCC. He said civilian protections in urban combat ultimately come down to the individual soldier making the right decision. "We just have to train on it," he said.[326]

In al-Nasiriyya, a change in or confusion about the rules of engagement may again have contributed to the civilian toll. A Marine officer, who came in a second wave, said al-Nasiriyya was the only place along the road to Baghdad declared "hostile." "In the combat zone, it meant anyone there was a bad guy," he said. Another Marine, who was among the first in al-Nasiriyya, said the ROE there were positive identification. During a daylong ambush further north near al-Shatra, however, the ROE were lifted and troops were told to "shoot anything that moves."

Conclusion and Recommendations

Contradictions between written and verbal rules of engagement have the potential to lead to civilian casualties and violations of international humanitarian law. While U.S. rules of engagement on paper met international humanitarian law standards, in practice, soldiers and Marines reported conflicting interpretations of what they meant and how to apply them in practice, particularly in the fighting in Baghdad and al-Nasiriyya, where most civilian casualties occurred. Further investigation would be required to determine if there were violations of IHL, but there is clearly a need for better guidance and training to reduce civilian casualties in future ground wars.

Human Rights Watch recommends:

- The U.S. military ensure that there is no confusion between written and verbal rules of engagement and that ROE are distributed in a timely fashion.

- Armed forces devote better training to application of rules of engagement, especially in urban warfare and in circumstances where the enemy may be wearing civilian clothes.

---

[325] Human Rights Watch telephone interview with Colonel Lyle Cayce.

[326] Human Rights Watch interview with Colonel David Perkins.

IV. EXPLOSIVE REMNANTS OF WAR

The impact of the war in Iraq on civilians did not end with the conclusion of major hostilities. Staggering quantities of explosive remnants of war continue to endanger civilians as well as military forces.[327] The Coalition's air and ground campaigns littered the country with tens of thousands of unexploded submunitions. These *de facto* landmines, which can detonate on contact, caused daily casualties in the weeks after the end of active hostilities and present lingering dangers in populated areas and open fields. Iraqi military and fedayeen forces abandoned large caches of weapons and ammunition in schools, mosques, hospitals, and residential neighborhoods. These munitions have killed or injured scores of Iraqis, many of whom are children, searching for scrap metal or playing with explosives. Opposition fighters have also looted the sites and used the ordnance for attacks on Coalition forces and against civilians, such as the deadly truck bombing at the U.N. headquarters in Baghdad on August 19.

The significant and ongoing impact of these explosive remnants of war demonstrates the need for armed forces to consider the post-attack effects of their actions. Belligerents should not use weapons with high dud rates or unnecessarily store weapons caches in civilian areas. After the conflict, they should ensure that unexploded ordnance and landmine locations are marked and cleared as soon as possible and that abandoned munition sites are secured quickly.

Cluster Munitions and the Dangers of Duds

Cluster munitions cause humanitarian harm not only because they are area effect weapons, but also because a large percentage of their bomblets or grenades do not explode on impact.[328] These explosive duds remain live and dangerous and are frequently set off by civilians after the strikes. In Iraq, they continue to cause deaths and injuries months after major fighting ended. Human Rights Watch documented hundreds of casualties with site visits, hospital records, and interviews with victims. Duds have also interfered with local agriculture. During the war, they impeded Coalition troop movements, and they have killed Coalition troops both during and after hostilities.

---

[327] Explosive remnants of war include all types of unexploded ordnance, which is ordnance that has been used but failed to explode, like cluster munition duds, and abandoned explosive ordnance, which has been left behind by parties to a conflict but not used. This chapter focuses on cluster munition duds and abandoned ordnance and does not address other types of ERW.

[328] Air-dropped submunitions are often called bomblets. Ground-launched submunitions are often called grenades.

The humanitarian and military harm they cause has led even some of the soldiers who fought in Iraq to call for an alternative to a weapon that produces so many duds.

Civilian Harm

The number of submunitions used in Iraq dwarfs that used in Afghanistan or Yugoslavia and has resulted in significant civilian casualties, after as well as during attacks.[329] Based on CENTCOM's reported 10,782 munitions, U.S. forces probably used at least 1.8 million submunitions; an average dud rate of 5 percent would leave about 90,000 duds.[330] The U.S. Air Force alone reported dropping about 1,206 cluster bombs containing 237,546 bomblets.[331] The British dropped seventy RBL-755 bombs containing 10,290 bomblets.[332] Dud rates vary by type of cluster bomb but even a conservative 5 percent dud rate would leave more than 12,000 unexploded bomblets. Ground-launched submunitions, which the Coalition did not use in Afghanistan or Yugoslavia, left even more duds, especially in populated areas. The U.S. Army and Marines have not revealed the number they used, but it is likely to be significantly higher than the number of air-dropped submunitions. In Karbala' alone, for example, a Marine explosive ordnance disposal team cleared 4,000 duds in less than a month.[333] The British reported firing 2,100 artillery-delivered cluster munitions in the area of Basra.[334] These L20A1s contained 102,900 grenades with a reported 2 percent dud rate.[335] While submunitions have caused civilian casualties in past conflicts, the large quantities used, heavy targeting of urban areas, and deployment of ground as well as air models magnified their impact in Iraq.

Ground-launched submunitions have caused the most post-conflict civilian casualties. Coalition forces used them extensively as part of unobserved counter-battery fire. Since

---

[329] During their air campaign in Yugoslavia from March to June 1999, NATO forces dropped about 1,765 cluster bombs containing about 295,000 bomblets. In Afghanistan between October 2001 and March 2002, the U.S. Air Force dropped about 1,228 cluster bombs containing 248,056 bomblets. Human Rights Watch, "Fatally Flawed," pp. 41, 1.

[330] For an explanation of how these numbers were calculated, see Ground-Launched Cluster Munitions section in the Conduct of the Ground War chapter above.

[331] "Operation Iraqi Freedom—By the Numbers," p. 11. As explained above, the United States also used JSOWs and TLAMs, which can contain submunitions, but it did not report how many of the ones used in Iraq carried that payload.

[332] U.K. Ministry of Defence, "Operations in Iraq—First Reflections."

[333] Human Rights Watch interview with Gunnery Sergeant Tracey Jones.

[334] Ann Treneman, "Mapped: The Lethal Legacy of Cluster Bombs."

[335] Thomas Frank, "Officials: Hundreds of Iraqis Killed by Faulty Grenades" (citing the British Ministry of Defence).

Iraqi forces often occupied populated areas on the edges of towns, the attacks left thousands of duds in urban neighborhoods and villages near the major cities of Iraq.

The post-strike situation in al-Hilla exemplifies the dangers MLRS and artillery duds pose civilians. Dr. al-Falluji at al-Hilla General Teaching Hospital said the city suffered almost daily casualties from clusters in the weeks after battle there.[336] From April 1 to April 11, the hospital recorded 221 war-related injuries mostly from duds. The hospital recorded an additional thirty-one injuries attributable to cluster duds from May through August.[337]

Explosive duds have endangered al-Hilla's inhabitants since moments after the battle began on March 31. Ambulances could not enter one neighborhood to evacuate wounded civilians because their drivers feared running over a dud in the dark; the next morning hundreds of injured civilians were taken to the hospital.[338] Three days later, in the village of al-Maimira, just southeast of town, a dud killed Hussain `Abbas, 30. "He prayed and had dinner and went inside his house," said `Abbas's sister. "Suddenly there was an explosion. He called, 'Rihab' [the name of his wife] and after that he died."[339] Duds in al-Kifl, a little further south, sent other civilians to al-Hilla Hospital. Thirteen-year-old Falah Hassan was injured by an unexploded DPICM on March 26 and remained in the hospital on May 19 awaiting skin grafts.[340] The explosion ripped off his right hand and spread shrapnel through his body. He also lost soft tissue in his lower limbs and his left index finger. His mother, who lay in the hospital bed next to his, suffered injuries to her abdomen, uterus, and large and small intestines from the same explosion.[341] In mid-May, long after the battle ended, cluster duds still threatened al-Hilla's people. A home in the Nadir neighborhood had two live DPICMs on its roof and second-floor terrace. Human Rights Watch also witnessed a young boy pick up a live dud and carry it down the street through a crowd of his neighbors. Fortunately, it did not explode.

---

[336] Human Rights Watch interview with Dr. Sa`ad al-Falluji.

[337] Al-Hilla General Teaching Hospital, War-Related Casualty Records.

[338] Human Rights Watch interview with Hussain Jabir, director, Civil Defense, al-Hilla, May 21, 2003.

[339] Human Rights Watch interview with sister of Hussain `Abbas, al-Maimira, May 20, 2003.

[340] Human Rights Watch interview with Falah Hassan, al-Hilla, May 19, 2003. The explosion injured three relatives, including his mother.

[341] Human Rights Watch interview with Dr. Sa`ad al-Falluji.

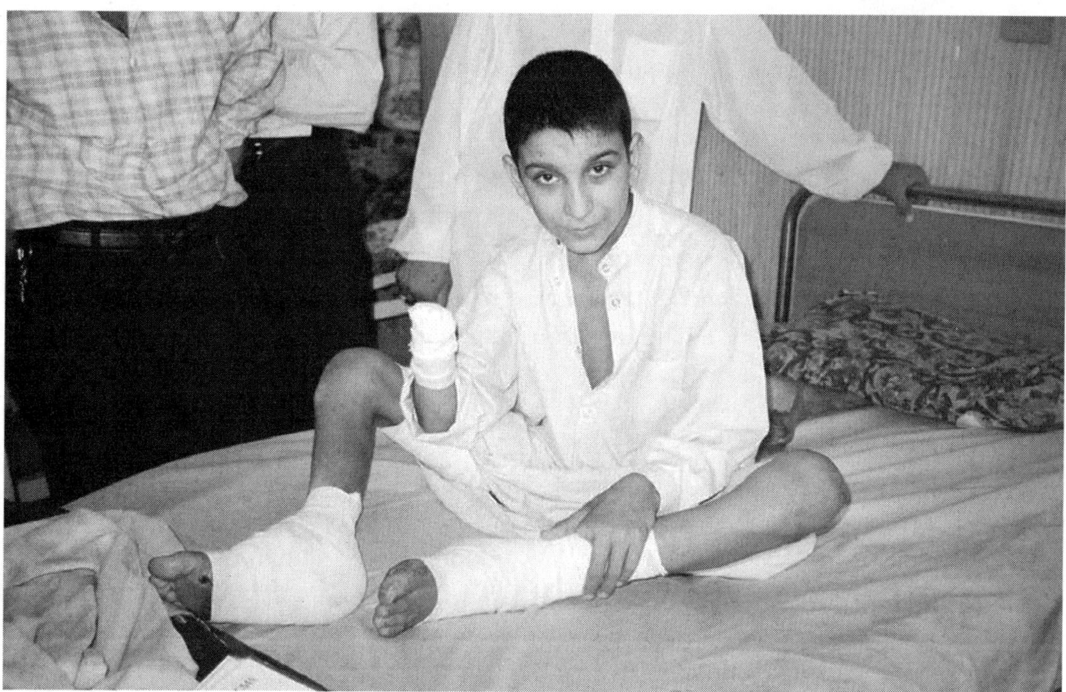

Falah Hassan, 13, was injured by an unexploded ground-launched submunition on March 26 and remained in al-Hilla General Teaching Hospital awaiting skin grafts on May 19. The explosion ripped off his right hand and spread shrapnel through his body. © 2003 Bonnie Docherty / Human Rights Watch

Civilians in other cities now occupied by U.S. forces suffered numerous casualties from duds. Al-Najaf Teaching Hospital treated 109 injured civilians, including twenty-eight children, in the week after the main battle for al-Najaf, most of whom were hurt by submunitions.[342] Several patients at that hospital described how they were injured and maimed by cluster duds. On March 26, Samir Qassim `Abbas, a 24-year-old taxi driver and college student, went to pick up some passengers in Abu Sukhair, fifteen kilometers (nine miles) east of al-Najaf. "I entered a house where I found something that looked like a piece of lamp. I kicked this thing. When I kicked, it exploded and I fell down," `Abbas said.[343] Two months later, he remained in the hospital. The submunition, which he identified from photographs as a Hydra dud, left him with injuries and bone loss in both legs. The right leg required skin grafts, and his left leg needed surgery to replace his tibia.[344] In al-Nasiriyya, three boys were injured by a DPICM at 10:00 a.m.

---

[342] Al-Najaf Teaching Hospital, War-Related Casualty Records, obtained by Human Rights Watch, al-Najaf, May 24, 2003.

[343] Human Rights Watch interview with Samir Qassim `Abbas, al-Najaf, May 24, 2003.

[344] Human Rights Watch interview with Dr. Muhammad Hassan al-`Ubaidi.

on April 28. Yasir Hamid, 11, suffered mild burns and his brother Hussain Hamid, 7, fractured his leg. Their cousin and neighbor, Mahir Qandil, 11, was also injured.[345]

U.K. submunitions posed similar threats in the south. In the Kam Sabil district of Basra, a strike left five duds on the roofs of civilian homes. A 9-year-old girl picked up one of the submunitions causing an explosion that killed her and injured her pregnant mother and 18-month-old brother.[346] Although the residents of al-Tannuma did not report any injuries from duds, submunitions from British L20A1s littered their neighborhood in Basra weeks after the war. Mechanic Mustafa `Abd al-Hassan, 45, found three duds in the yard of his home when he returned after the attack.[347] The British cleared two, but a third remained at the end of May. It lay at the base of the back wall of his house with only cans of cooking oil to mark its location.

While ground-launched submunitions have caused the overwhelming majority of the post-combat cluster casualties in Iraq, air-dropped cluster bombs have also contributed to the number of civilian deaths and injuries. The latter have caused fewer casualties, in part, because the U.S. Air Force learned a lesson from past wars and limited the number of cluster bombs it used in or near civilian areas. It did make exceptions, however, that left duds in residential neighborhoods. In Baghdad, for example, the U.S. Air Force dropped cluster bombs on a date farm in Hay Tunis. The Iraqi military had used the grove to hide military vehicles, thus making it a legitimate target for the United States, but immediately across the street, on at least two sides, were densely populated residential areas. Two days after the attack in early April, Hussam Jasmi, 13, and Muhammad Mun`im Muhammad, 14, cousins who lived a few minutes away from the farm, stepped on a BLU-97 submunition. The bomblet ripped off their legs and ultimately killed them.[348] The U.S. military came to clear the farm around May 13, but later that week, Human Rights Watch still found bomblets on the site.

---

[345] Human Rights Watch interview with Hamid `Atshan, al-Nasiriyya, May 7, 2003. `Atshan, 36, is the father of Yasir and Hussain Hamid.

[346] Human Rights Watch interview with international aid worker #2, Basra, May 1, 2003.

[347] Human Rights Watch interview with Mustafa `Abd al-Hassan, Basra, May 30, 2003.

[348] Human Rights Watch interview with Muhammad `Abd Mamon, Baghdad, May 17, 2003. Mamon, 32, was the uncle of the two boys.

al-Tannuma: School and Neighborhood Hit by U.K. Cluster Munitions
Field with Iraqi Tanks
School
Home of Mustafa `Abd al-Hassan
Homes
Cluster Strikes (HRW Data)
Basra
Satellite Image: Space Imaging
Photographed September 20, 2001
0
50
100
200
Meters
N

Unexploded bomblets also endanger civilians in more rural areas. Najat Khalid lost her two sons to BLU-97s in the village of Sichir near al-Falluja. Neighbor Kayun Risham, 50, was injured.[349] Military vehicles located near the farms where they lived may have been legitimate military targets. The large number of duds left by the weapon chosen, however, unnecessarily endangered civilians.

Children are particularly vulnerable to unexploded submunitions, regardless of the type. "Bomblets are what kids pick up. There is a nice ribbon on the end [of a DPICM]. It's nice for carrying," said an officer at the Baghdad Civil-Military Operations Center (CMOC).[350] `Abbas Hussain, 12, for example, lost half of his hand to a cluster grenade. "He picked up something in the road. He thought it was something to play with, but it hit the ground and exploded," said Hussain's uncle Hossam al-`Alawi during an interview at al-Najaf Teaching Hospital. To make matters worse, Hussain is a hemophiliac.[351] Doctors around Iraq agreed that children were the most common victims of cluster duds. "Cluster bombs sometimes look like beautiful things. Children like to play with them. [The duds] are here and there, everywhere on farmland. They look shiny," said Dr. al-`Ubaidi at al-Najaf Teaching Hospital.[352] Hospital records provide additional evidence of this trend. Fifty-six children (25 percent of the casualties) were injured in al-Hilla in April; twenty-eight children (26 percent of the casualties) were injured the first week after the battle of al-Najaf.

Abandoned Iraqi submunitions have also endangered civilians. According to the CMOC officer in Baghdad, cluster casualties were caused by a "combination of the ones we fired and Iraqi artillery stores spread around." He said U.S. troops had encountered KB-1s, a Yugoslavian version of a DPICM submunition, left by the Iraqis.[353] Some of these submunitions may have been ejected when their canisters were hit by fire. In al-`Amara, near Basra, six people died from such ordnance. "Kids were playing with Iraqi MLRS," said Warrant Officer 1 Nick Pettit of the British Joint Force EOD Group.[354]

---

[349] Human Rights Watch interview with `Abdul-Runaima, Sichir, May 14, 2003. Runaima, who lives on the chicken farm where CBU-103s were dropped, is the brother of Risham and neighbor of Khalid.

[350] Human Rights Watch interview with CMOC officer, Baghdad, May 13, 2003.

[351] Human Rights Watch interview with Hossam al-`Alawi, al-Najaf, May 24, 2003.

[352] Human Rights Watch interview with Dr. Muhammad Hassan al-`Ubaidi.

[353] Human Rights Watch interview with CMOC officer.

[354] Human Rights Watch interview with Warrant Officer 1 Nick Pettit, Joint Forces EOD Group, 33 Engineers Regiment, Corps of Royal Engineers, British Army, Basra, May 28, 2003.

Duds from Coalition cluster munitions not only cause civilian casualties but also interfere with agriculture and the economic recovery of Iraq. Both air- and ground-launched cluster munitions litter fields along the battle route to Baghdad. The U.S. Air Force dropped CBUs on an Iraqi military position across from the Agargouf ziggurat. The field contained an SA-3 surface-to-air missile battery and radar truck. In May, dozens of unexploded BLU-97 bomblets still covered the field, some lying in ditches where they had fallen or been placed by locals, others buried in the ground after piercing the soft surface on impact. While Human Rights Watch was investigating the site, a shepherd, apparently oblivious to the danger, walked through with a flock of about forty sheep and goats. They grazed among the bomblets, and one goat nibbled grass with a BLU between its legs. About half an hour later, while at another part of the site, the Human Rights Watch team heard a large explosion from the cluster bomb field, possibly a bomblet set off by one of the animals.

Cluster grenades interfere even more with agriculture. DPICMs and ATACMS submunitions littered farmland in the month after the war, and in some places, like Agargouf, were found in close proximity to air-dropped bomblets. "We have to burn the fields. There are still bombs there. We are growing grains for our animals," said the father of Falah Hassan, the submunition victim from al-Kifl.[355] In May, Human Rights Watch found fields contaminated with submunitions in villages around al-Hilla, al-Najaf, al-Falluja, and Agargouf.

Adverse Military Consequences

While the broad footprint of a cluster munition has military value, the numerous duds do not. These unexploded submunitions are not intentionally left behind; they fail to explode as designed. In Iraq, cluster duds not only decreased the effectiveness of the weapon against enemy troops but also endangered Coalition troops and interfered with some military operations.

Unexploded submunitions have killed at least five members of the Coalition military. On March 27, Marine Lance Corporal Jesus A. Suarez del Solar, 20, died after stepping on an unexploded submunition in a field near Baghdad.[356] A few weeks later on April 19, an Iraqi girl handed Army Sergeant Troy Jenkins of the 101st Airborne Division a cluster grenade, which exploded injuring several soldiers in the area. Jenkins, 25, died

---

[355] Human Rights Watch interview with father of Falah Hassan, al-Hilla, May 19, 2003.

[356] Blanca Gonzalez, "Mexican-Born Marine Killed near Baghdad to Be Buried in Peace, Father Says," Copley News Service, April 4, 2003; "Father of Slain Soldier Leads Anti-War Rally; Man Says Latinos Need More Opportunities outside Military," Associated Press, May 24, 2003.

from his injuries four days later.[357] The United Kingdom has also lost troops to unexploded submunitions. Lieutenant Colonel Shanahan of the British Joint Force EOD Group reported that three soldiers were killed while clearing submunitions in Basra. A fourth suffered injuries from a cluster grenade that exploded fifty meters (fifty-five yards) away from him.[358]

Duds have also interfered with some military operations. Colonel Baldwin of the Queen's Dragoon Guards encountered a field of DPICMs west of Umm Qasr, 500 meters (.3 miles) north of the Kuwaiti border. "The first night [of the war], the lead vehicle of our convoy walked straight into a cluster bomb field. The corporal came out white faced. . . . It took half an hour to get out," he said.[359] In some cases, units chose not to use cluster munitions because they knew their own troops would have to cross a field littered with duds.[360] Such incidents demonstrate how cluster munitions can be detrimental to the military as well as civilians. Reducing the dud rate is thus a place where military necessity and humanitarian concern coincide.

New Technology

Both the United States and United Kingdom deployed new types of cluster munitions in Iraq that are designed to reduce the dud rate. The U.S. Air Force dropped the CBU-105 Sensor Fuzed Weapon for the first time in combat. This weapon, eighty-eight of which were used, employs the Wind Corrected Munitions Dispenser. It contains ten BLU-108 submunitions, each of which releases four skeet warheads, the size of hockey pucks, with infrared sensors.[361] To reduce the dud rate, the submunitions have self-destruct mechanisms.[362] Human Rights Watch visited one site outside of al-Hilla where the United States had dropped CBU-105s on an isolated field of artillery. No unexploded

---

[357] Valerie Alvord, Debbie Howlett, and Tom Kenworthy, "Lingering Dangers Claim Four in Iraq," *USA Today*, April 29, 2003; Thomas Frank, "Officials: Hundreds of Iraqis Killed By Faulty Grenades." The press reported several different versions of the story, and Chairman of the Joint Chiefs of Staff General Richard Myers denied that the ordnance was a submunition. Jenkins' fellow soldiers, however, told a reporter in September they believed it was a DPICM because of the ballistic evidence they found at the scene. They also had been clearing one hundred DPICMs a day at the time of the accident. E-mail message from Paul Wiseman, *USA Today*, to Bonnie Docherty, Human Rights Watch, September 10, 2003.

[358] Human Rights Watch interview with Lieutenant Colonel John Shanahan.

[359] Human Rights Watch telephone interview with Colonel Gil Baldwin.

[360] Human Rights Watch interview with U.S. Marine officer #2, Iraq, May 2003.

[361] As discussed in the Conduct of the Air War chapter, the CBU-105 has a WCMD guidance system to increase accuracy, and each individual skeet has an infrared sensor to target armored vehicles.

[362] Global Security.org, "BLU-108/B Submunition," January 19, 2003, http://www.globalsecurity.org/military/systems/munitions/blu-108.htm (retrieved October 22, 2003).

skeets were visible although some could have been hidden in the tall grass. The CBU-105 Sensor Fuzed Weapon is a potentially significant development that attempts to address key humanitarian problems associated with cluster weapons: accuracy of both the munition and submunition and dud rates. Further investigation should be done to calculate its dud rate in actual combat operations and determine if it meets its design standards in practice.

The United States also for the first time used two CBU-107s, which contain 3,700 non-explosive rods. It dropped them on the Ministry of Information in order to destroy rooftop antennae. This weapon has the advantage of not leaving explosive duds. Further investigations should be done to determine its overall humanitarian effect.

In a U.K. combat first, British forces used the L20A1, an artillery shell with M85 submunitions similar to U.S. DPICMs but with self-destruct mechanisms.[363] The submunition has a dud rate of 2 percent, according to the British Ministry of Defense.[364] If that rate occurs in actual combat, it would be an improvement over the U.S. model, which has a reported 14 percent dud rate.[365] Human Rights Watch could not determine the rate from the field, but it did find evidence of duds from L20A1s in multiple areas of Basra. In al-Tannuma, for example, three unexploded submunitions lay in Mustafa `Abd al-Hassan's yard when he returned to his home the morning after the strike. One of those had been buried under garbage and missed by British EOD teams; it was still in his yard on May 30.[366] Other civilians in the neighborhood reported duds left by the attack. Tha'ir Zaidan, 25, said, "I carried one in my hand across the street. I set it down carefully and made a sign. It was between my kids. I had no choice."[367] He found another grenade in his house. Across Shatt al-`Arab river, U.N. deminers found a grenade that was probably from an L20A1 on the roof of their new headquarters, in a clearly populated area.[368] Ironically the promise of a lower dud rate may have made the British less careful about where they used the L20A1. "There was less of a reluctance to

---

[363] The Israelis have already used this munition in southern Lebanon.

[364] Thomas Frank, "Officials: Hundreds of Iraqis Killed by Faulty Grenades" (citing the British Ministry of Defence).

[365] U.S. Army Defense Ammunition Center, Technical Center for Explosives Safety, "Study of Ammunition Dud and Low Order Detonation Rates," p. 9.

[366] Human Rights Watch interview with Mustafa `Abd al-Hassan.

[367] Human Rights Watch interview with Tha'ir Zaidan.

[368] Human Rights Watch interview with Bill Van Ree, team leader, U.N. Mine Action Coordination Team (UNMACT), Basra, May 29, 2003.

use them because of the increased reliability," Colonel Baldwin said.[369] Efforts to reduce the dud rate of cluster munitions should be commended; however, the rates must be made significantly lower and cluster munitions must be kept out of populated areas if humanitarian harm is to be minimized.

Despite the availability of new technology, the Coalition continued to use old cluster munitions with high dud rates. The U.S. and U.K. air forces both dropped versions of the Vietnam-era Rockeye. The weapon had been used extensively in the 1991 Gulf War and its duds are still being cleared. While no reliable estimate of the failure rate is available, clearance agencies in Kuwait encountered a very large number of dud Rockeye submunitions in their operations.[370] One U.S. company reported clearing 95,799 Mk-118 Rockeye duds in its sector of Kuwait, which constituted 18 percent of the total area cleared.[371] In 2002, 451 Rockeye duds were detected and destroyed by mine clearance and explosive ordnance disposal teams in Kuwait.[372]

Growing Opposition to Cluster Munitions

The humanitarian harm and military impediments caused by cluster munition duds compelled even Coalition forces in Iraq to join those who question use of the weapon. International concern about submunitions' negative impact on civilians has increased steadily in recent years.[373] Human Rights Watch, for example, called for a moratorium on use of cluster munitions until the humanitarian concerns associated with the weapon are addressed.[374] Responding to external and internal pressure, the U.S. Air Force, which used cluster bombs in the 1991 Gulf War, Yugoslavia, and Afghanistan, has modified its practices to reduce, although not eliminate, the weapons' impact on civilians. For example, it dropped fewer cluster bombs in populated areas and used

---

[369] Human Rights Watch telephone interview with Colonel Gil Baldwin.

[370] Colin King, "Explosive Remnants of War: A Study on Submunitions and Other Unexploded Ordnance," report commissioned by the ICRC, August 2000, pp. 16, E-2; U.S. General Accounting Office, "Military Operations: Information on U.S. Use of Land Mines in the Persian Gulf War," GAO-02-1003, September 2002, p. 27. A Department of Defense report to Congress in 2000 cites a 98 percent submunition reliability rate for the Rockeye submunition—a claim not supported by the Kuwait evidence. Office of the Under Secretary of Defense for Acquisition, Technology, and Logistics, "Unexploded Ordnance Report," table 2-3, p. 5.

[371] U.S. Army Armament, Munitions, and Chemical Command, "Contract DAAA21-92-M-0300 Report by CMS, Inc.," n.d.

[372] Compiled from Kuwait Ministry of Defense, "Monthly Ammunition and Explosive Destroyed/Recovery Reports," December 2001-December 2002, Annex A.

[373] For a discussion of the public debate about cluster bombs in Afghanistan, see Human Rights Watch, "Fatally Flawed," pp. 16-19.

[374] Human Rights Watch, Memorandum to Convention on Conventional Weapons (CCW) Delegates.

primarily newer models. The war in Iraq was the first in a decade to involve large numbers of U.S. and U.K. ground forces. Their combat experiences with artillery and MLRS submunitions led some soldiers and Marines to call for an alternative weapon with fewer deadly side effects.

Several Army and Marine officers interviewed by Human Rights Watch said they felt uncomfortable using a weapon that produced so many duds and called for the development of a better alternative. "We have to demand giving commanders better options," said Lieutenant Colonel Stephen Baer, operations officer for the Third Infantry Division, noting the danger duds pose to soldiers passing through the strike areas.[375] Leaders of the division's Second Brigade expressed a reluctance to use cluster munitions. "We had concerns about unexploded ordnance. . . . It's a constant consideration. What are the second or third effects?" said commanding officer Colonel Perkins.[376] In some cases, his brigade sought less harmful alternatives. When calling for close air support, he said it preferred JDAMs or an A10 "Warthog" with tank-killing close air support. In Baghdad, it used high explosive artillery airbursts over highway clover leafs to reduce damage to the roads. For longer-range ground support, however, the MLRS is "the only type of munition we have."[377] The MLRS, which uses submunitions exclusively and has a dud rate of 16 percent,[378] was the only weapon available at the divisional level with a range of thirty-two kilometers (twenty miles), or if an extended range model, forty-five kilometers (twenty-eight miles). When the division offered it, however, "we wouldn't always use it," Perkins said.[379]

A post-conflict lessons learned presentation by the Third Infantry Division echoed the concerns of its field officers. The division described dud-producing submunitions, particularly the DPICM, as among the "losers" of the war. "Is DPICM munition a Cold War relic?" the presentation asked. The dud rate of the DPICM, which represented more than half of its direct support battalion's available arsenal, was higher than expected, especially when not used on roads. Commanders were "hesitant to use it . . . but had to." The presentation specifically noted that these weapons are "not for use in urban areas."[380]

---

[375] Human Rights Watch interview with Lieutenant Colonel Stephen Baer.

[376] Human Rights Watch interview with Colonel David Perkins.

[377] Ibid.

[378] Office of the Under Secretary of Defense for Acquisition, Technology, and Logistics, "Unexploded Ordnance Report," table 2-3, p. 5.

[379] Human Rights Watch interview with Colonel David Perkins.

[380] Third Infantry Division, "Fires in the Close Fight: OIF [Operation Iraqi Freedom] Lessons Learned."

Marines in the field also complained about the aftereffects of submunitions. "The biggest UXO [unexploded ordnance] problem is clusters because they are extremely sensitive and were used extensively. We wouldn't use cluster bombs in battle even if it degraded [our capacity]," said one Marine on condition of anonymity.[381] The development of an alternative to cluster munitions would protect the lives of both civilians and soldiers. It would also decrease the cost of clearing duds after the conflict.

Conclusion and Recommendations

The aftereffects of cluster munitions raise concerns under international humanitarian law. As explained above, an attack will be unlawfully disproportionate if it "may be expected to cause incidental loss of civilian life, injury to civilians, damage to civilian objects, or a combination thereof, which would be excessive in relation to the concrete and military advantage anticipated."[382] If this proportionality test is interpreted as encompassing more than immediate losses, the large number of explosive duds may make cluster munition use disproportionate. Taking into account both strike and post-strike casualties greatly increases the likelihood that the loss would be excessive in relation to the military advantage, especially if an attack occurred in a populated area or an area to which people might return. The U.S. Air Force has said that the dud rate must be part of the proportionality determination because unexploded bomblets are "reasonably foreseeable."[383]

Because of their duds, cluster munitions also exemplify weapons that can be indiscriminate in effect. Indiscriminate attacks include those that "employ a method or means of combat the effects of which cannot" distinguish between military targets and civilian objects.[384] Even if a cluster munition *strike* is not indiscriminate, its *effects* may be. The effects become more dangerous if the submunitions litter an area frequented by civilians or the dud rate is high due to poor design, use in inappropriate environments, or delivery from a high altitude. Cluster duds cannot distinguish between combatants and civilians and will likely injure or kill whoever disturbs them. Under either the proportionality test or the indiscriminate effects provision, the high dud rate of cluster

---

[381] Human Rights Watch interview with U.S. Marine officer #2.

[382] Protocol I, art. 51(5)(b).

[383] U.S. Air Force, Bullet Background Paper on International Legal Aspects Concerning the Use of Cluster Munitions.

[384] Protocol I, art. 51(4)(c).

munitions combined with the large number of submunitions they release challenges the principle of distinction.

As discussed above, states are required to minimize civilian harm. Given the potential indiscriminateness discussed above, the United States, and other countries that use cluster munitions, should avoid strikes in or near populated areas and minimize the long-term effects of duds.[385] The availability of alternative weapons should also be considered.

The situation in Iraq highlights the need to suspend the use of cluster munitions until the dud rate is dramatically reduced. Although the proportionality test necessitates a case-by-case analysis, in general, the extensive aftereffects of Coalition cluster grenades in or near populated areas call for close scrutiny under this provision. The large number of duds and their serious and long-term impact on civilian life and livelihoods also suggest that at least some models of submunitions, when used in or near populated areas, are indiscriminate in effect. Finally, the United States and others may not have taken "all feasible precautions" to reduce the dud rate. The British use of L20A1s shows that self-destruct weapons are available for use in the field, and on paper, the United States has recognized the value of that technology. In 2001, the U.S. Secretary of Defense William Cohen stated that all future submunitions must have a dud rate of less than 1 percent.[386] In August 2003, General Richard Myers, chairman of the Joint Chiefs of Staff, said the Army planned to use self-destruct fuzes on some DPICMs in 2005.[387] In the meantime, however, the United States littered Iraq with outdated, unreliable submunitions. Militaries planning for future battles in urban or populated areas must consider changes in targeting and technology that will make the use of cluster munitions less problematic.

To address the dangers of cluster munition duds, Human Rights Watch recommends that:

---

[385] Human Rights Watch, "Fatally Flawed," p. 12.

[386] Secretary of Defense William Cohen, Memorandum for the Secretaries of the Military Departments, Subject: Department of Defense Policy on Submunition Reliability (U), January 10, 2001.

[387] General Richard B. Myers, Chairman, Joint Chiefs of Staff, to Senator Patrick Leahy, August 11, 2003. Myers said the U.S. Army plans to add a self-destruct fuze to the 155mm extended range DPICM in 2005. It "is also developing a self-destruct fuze to reduce the dud rate to below 1 percent for its cluster munitions in rocket and other cannon artillery systems. This new fuze may be available for future production of Army cluster munitions as soon as 2005." Ibid.

- The use of submunitions should be suspended until the initial dud rate can be reduced dramatically, at least to less than 1 percent.

- Whatever the dud rate, armed forces should consider the long-term effects of cluster munitions when choosing targets. Cluster munitions should not be used in populated areas where the risk of civilian casualties from duds increases.

- The United States, the United Kingdom, and others should continue efforts to improve the reliability of submunitions. They should also consider if weapons with fewer humanitarian side effects can replace them.

- To facilitate post-conflict clearance of duds, armed forces, especially U.S. ground forces, should improve their recording of cluster strikes and share that information with deminers and the public.

Abandoned Explosive Ordnance

As they retreated from the Coalition advance, Iraqi forces abandoned massive quantities of explosive ordnance that they had stored in populated residential areas. These arms and ammunition—most outdated and many unstable—caused scores of civilian casualties both during combat operations and afterwards, and they continue to endanger the civilian population today. The abandoned explosive ordnance has presented deadly temptations to children looking for entertainment and adults searching for goods to use or sell. It has also served as a munitions source for those opposing the Coalition, some of whom have targeted civilians. U.S. and British forces failed to secure or clear these abandoned munition sites in a timely fashion, most notably in Basra and Baghdad, and thus bear some of the responsibility for the numerous civilian deaths and injuries. During the remainder of their occupation of Iraq and in similar situations in the future, Coalition forces should prioritize securing abandoned munitions for the safety of the local population, international aid and U.N. workers, and their own troops.

There may be more than 600,000 tons of abandoned munitions throughout Iraq, according to the director general of the National Mine Action Authority in Iraq.[388] Coalition troops repeatedly remarked on the extent of the abandoned munition problem in Iraq. "We inherited a city full of ordnance," said a CMOC officer in Baghdad. "The big problem in terms of quantity is not bomblets, but crates and crates of explosive ordnance."[389] Lieutenant Colonel Tim Everhard of the U.S. Third Ordnance Battalion,

---

[388] "Letter from the National Mine Action Authority in Iraq, by Siraj Barzani, Director General, October 9, 2003," printed in Mine Action Support Group October Newsletter, New York, October 2003, p. 24, http://maic.jmu.edu/journals/masg/MASG%20NewsLetter%20October2003.doc (November 13, 2003).

[389] Human Rights Watch interview with CMOC officer.

who was in charge of Coalition clearance efforts in the capital, echoed this statement. He said his teams had received reports of 400 caches in Baghdad alone. "We are finding everything. You can't swing a dead cat in Baghdad without hitting an RPG," Everhard said.[390] While unguarded caches represent the biggest humanitarian threat, isolated explosive ordnance also litters the country. Human Rights Watch found a stray RPG in the middle of a Baghdad traffic circle at the foot of the statue of King Faisal.

The situation in the British sector in southern Iraq is similar, if not worse. "I've never seen so much ordnance, and I've been in the Balkans, Northern Iraq, and Afghanistan," said CMOC representative John Thompson.[391] Lieutenant Colonel Shanahan said he was "astounded by the amount of ordnance."[392]

Iraqi forces kept many of their stockpiles in or near populated areas, which magnified the danger to civilians. "It's hard. There are ammunition supply points in neighborhoods, in basements, in backyards. The condos by the airport are full of ordnance," Lieutenant Colonel Everhard said.[393] A representative from an international relief organization said he visited thirty schools in Basra and encountered abandoned stocks "everywhere."[394] Near al-Maqal Airfield in Basra, Human Rights Watch found a sprawling, unsecured storage facility a half kilometer (.3 miles) from residential neighborhoods. It included twenty-six partially buried shipping containers housing millions of rounds of anti-aircraft ammunition, thousands of anti-ship rounds, hundreds of air-to-air helicopter rockets, and hundreds of RPGs. Ironically, the Iraqi military could not use much of this ordnance. Most of it was old or incompatible with more recent Iraqi weapons; because it dates to the Soviet era, it lacks the safety designs of more modern munitions.[395]

---

[390] Human Rights Watch interview with Lieutenant Colonel Tim Everhard, commanding officer, Third Ordnance Battalion, U.S. Army, Baghdad, May 14, 2003.

[391] Human Rights Watch interview with John Thompson, CMOC representative, First U.K. Armoured Division, Basra, May 28, 2003.

[392] Human Rights Watch interview with Lieutenant Colonel John Shanahan.

[393] Human Rights Watch interview with Lieutenant Colonel Tim Everhard.

[394] Human Rights Watch interview with international aid worker #2.

[395] Human Rights Watch interview with Major Michael Samarov.

Iraqi forces abandoned this unsecured weapons cache near al-Maqal Airfield in northwest Basra. The munitions were strewn about by civilians trying to salvage scrap metal. Parts of this site spontaneously combusted in 120 degree Fahrenheit heat days after this photo was taken. © 2003 Marc Garlasco / Human Rights Watch

While stockpiling munitions in populated areas is part of urban warfare, Iraqi military and fedayeen stored their weapons in civilian buildings. "Ninety percent of their caches were stuck in hospitals, schools, and mosques," Lieutenant Colonel Everhard said. Fedayeen, for example, occupied the Surgical Hospital in al-Nasiriyya during the war. Hours after surrounding the building, U.S. Marines took 170 Iraqis captive and found 200 weapons, boxes and boxes of ammunition, 3,000 chemical warfare protection suits, and a tank in the hospital compound, officers said.[396] In early April 2003, Human Rights Watch learned that Iraqi forces had stored landmines inside a mosque in Qadir Karam in northern Iraq and laid mines around the mosque before abandoning it. The Mines Advisory Group removed 1,077 antivehicle and antipersonnel mines from the

---

[396] "Euphrates Battle May Be Biggest So Far," CNN.com, March 25, 2003, http://www.cnn.com/2003/WORLD/meast/03/25/sprj.irq.war.main/ (retrieved October 20, 2003).

site.[397] Human Rights Watch documented similar reports of munitions stored in hospitals and mosques from other troops involved in clearance of these sites.[398]

Dangers to Civilians

Abandoned Iraqi munition caches have caused significant civilian casualties. Many Iraqis try to scavenge scraps from such caches that they can then use at home or sell on the market. In some cases, they empty crates of ammunition for firewood and leave explosive ordnance spread across a site. In other cases, they remove the warheads of artillery shells in order to collect brass casings or gather propellant for fuel.[399] Both activities threaten the lives and limbs of the scavengers and leave explosive remnants that endanger future passersby.

Human Rights Watch found evidence of looting in regions occupied by U.S. and U.K. troops. In Karbala', during the third week of May, locals were scavenging at a fedayeen training center when an explosion collapsed the building, killing four civilians. "Sites like this will be a long-term problem," said Major Samarov. "Now the building is functionally booby-trapped."[400] At the Basra storage facility, looters left propellant strewn across the site and warheads lying in the open. Four days after Human Rights Watch's visit, one of the containers of unsealed ordnance "cooked off" with a huge explosion.[401] In Iraq's summer heat, scattered munitions do not need human intervention to detonate.

Children are frequent victims of abandoned munitions. On May 9 in Baghdad, Muhammad Keun Jiheli, 16, brought a piece of ordnance home to use for cooking fuel. An explosion killed four members of his family. He suffered burns over 72 percent of his body, and Jamil Salem Hamid, also 16, received burns over 54 percent of his body.[402] Munition caches also endanger children who think that lighting propellant is a game. Bill Van Ree of the U.N. Mine Action Coordination Team (UNMACT) said he saw "young

---

[397] Human Rights Watch, "Iraqi Mines Found in Mosque," Press Release, April 2, 2003.

[398] Human Rights Watch interview with CMOC officer (reporting on Baghdad); Human Rights Watch interview with Major Michael Samarov (reporting on Karbala').

[399] Human Rights Watch interview with Lieutenant Colonel John Shanahan.

[400] Human Rights Watch interview with Major Michael Samarov.

[401] Human Rights Watch interview with Danish Church Aid, Basra, May 28, 2003.

[402] Human Rights Watch interview with Ugo Bernieri, Relief Coordinator for the Italian Red Cross, Baghdad, May 14, 2003.

men" throwing matches on spilled ordnance in Basra and "having a great time."[403] At 2:00 p.m. on May 3, eight-year-old `Ali `Abdul-Amir put a match to a piece of explosive ordnance outside a school in al-Hay al-`Askari, a neighborhood of al-Nasiriyya. The explosion left him with burns and shrapnel injuries.[404] Human Rights Watch witnessed children playing among munitions and propellant at the large cache in Basra.

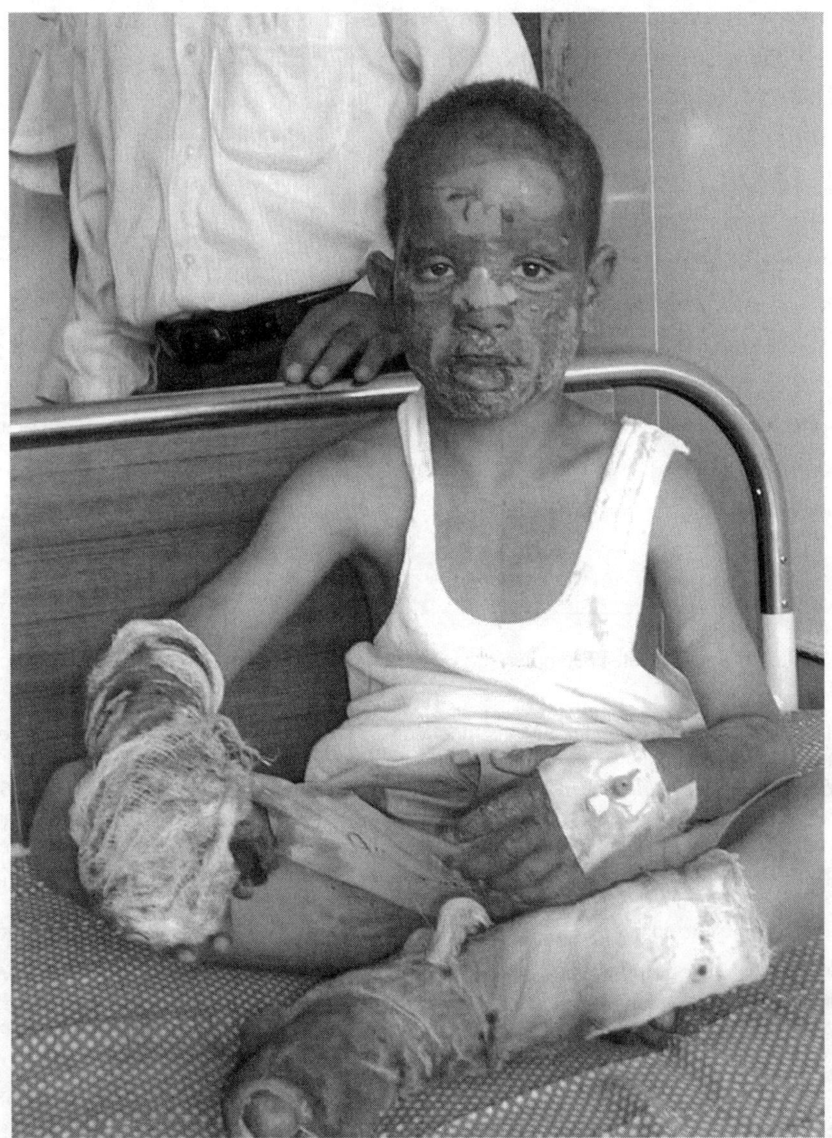

Eight-year-old `Ali `Abdul-Amir suffered severe burns and shrapnel injuries when he put a match to a piece of explosive ordnance outside his school in al-Nasiriyya. © 2003 Reuben E. Brigety, II / Human Rights Watch

[403] Human Rights Watch interview with Bill Van Ree, May 29, 2003.

[404] Human Rights Watch interview with `Abdul-Amir Matrud Lafta, al-Nasiriyya, May 7, 2003. Lafta, 47, was the victim's father.

Iraqi ammunition caches also endanger civilians because the materiel in arms caches is often still viable weaponry. At 4:45 p.m. on August 19, a truck bomb exploded at the Canal Hotel, the U.N. headquarters in Baghdad. The attack killed twenty-two civilians and injured scores more, including U.N. staff from Iraq and abroad and nongovernmental organization (NGO) visitors. Sergio Vieira de Mello, the U.N. special representative in Iraq and U.N. high commissioner for human rights, was among the dead. Investigations after the fact showed that the bomb had been made from old munitions.[405] The U.N. bombing was not an isolated incident. Ten days later, another blast, this time from a bomb in a van, killed ninety-one people at the Imam `Ali Shrine in al-Najaf. Investigators reported that this attack was "fueled with Soviet-era munitions likely scavenged from weapons depots belonging to the former Iraqi army."[406] Such attacks not only kill innocent Iraqis. They also threaten the future of humanitarian aid operations in Iraq. After the U.N. attack, 120 NGOs pulled out some of their staff, and the ICRC cut its international staff by two-thirds.[407] The number of U.N. foreign employees dropped from 600 before the attack to sixty by October 1.[408] Additional attacks on civilian targets, including the ICRC, led the United Nations to withdraw its entire international staff from Baghdad[409] and the ICRC to close its offices in Baghdad and Basra.[410]

---

[405] Christine Spolar, "FBI Can't Detect Common Signature in Five Major Iraqi Bomb Attacks," *Chicago Tribune*, September 17, 2003.

[406] Ibid. Iraqi officials also said that the munitions "could easily have been stolen from unguarded weapons depots." "Although U.S. military officials maintain that all known munitions sites have 'some level of protection,' Iraqi law-enforcement officials have found dozens of sites—including a vast facility about 35 miles [56 kilometers] outside Baghdad and another one 16 miles [26 kilometers] outside Najaf—so poorly guarded that scavengers are regularly seen rummaging through the weaponry. At the Najaf weapons site, at least one scavenger told a reporter that he could enter the grounds by bribing Iraqi guards the equivalent of $3. In Baghdad, law-enforcement officials who recently visited the site found no guards or barriers in place and hundreds of warheads exposed, many with their nose cones removed and their explosives in clear sight." Ibid.

[407] Harry de Quetteville and Sally Pook, "Frightened Aid Workers Set to Flee Iraq: 'We Are Used to Working in Theatres of War, but This Is Something Else,'" *Daily Telegraph*, September 1, 2003. See also Beatriz Lecumberri, "As U.N. Pulls Out of Iraq, NGOs Lose Heart," Agence France-Presse, September 26, 2003.

[408] "U.N. Pledges to Continue Working in Iraq," Agence France-Presse, October 1, 2003. "The staff of the United Nations and particularly the staff of the UNHCR, if they do not return to the country, this will have very deleterious consequences on a humanitarian level," Iraqi's interim Minister for Migration and Exiled Persons Mohammed Jassem Khudir told the U.N. high commissioner for refugees. Ibid.

[409] The pullout was a response to a car bombing that killed twelve people at the ICRC headquarters in Baghdad. "UN Says International Staff Are All out of Baghdad," U.N. News Service, November 6, 2003. In early November, the United Nations still had about forty international staff members in northern Iraq and 4,000 Iraqi staff members around the country. Ibid. See also Marc Carnegie, "Annan Vows Change as UN Moves Ahead with Iraq Pullout," Agence France-Presse, November 3, 2003.

[410] Sally Sara, "Red Cross Cuts Iraq Operation," Australian Broadcasting Corporation, November 9, 2003.

It is likely that those opposing the Coalition forces have also used these abandoned stockpiles to launch attacks. Since President Bush announced the end of major hostilities on May 1, both U.S. and U.K. forces have faced frequent attacks. As of November 11, 171 Coalition troops had died from hostile attacks after the end of major hostilities, more than the 142 who died during active combat.[411] It is unclear where those opposing the Coalition obtain their weapons and ammunition, but the abandoned munition caches are one likely source. Securing and clearing them is therefore an area where military and humanitarian concerns coincide.

Protection of Civilians

The United States and United Kingdom have a duty as occupying powers to protect the Iraqi people. With respect to abandoned explosive ordnance, this duty means securing sites immediately and clearing them as soon as possible. At the time of the Human Rights Watch mission, clearance was proceeding slowly but steadily while efforts to secure the sites were minimal.

The first priority for dealing with abandoned ordnance should have been securing sites. Keeping civilians away from caches, particularly large ones like the site in Basra that Human Rights Watch visited, removes the temptation to search for scraps or playthings and helps protect civilian lives. It also ensures that the ordnance does not end up in the hands of those that threaten both civilians—local and foreign—and Coalition troops. Finally, properly securing explosive ordnance sites facilitates later clearance by keeping the ordnance in its proper containers.

Human Rights Watch's investigation showed that six weeks after the end of major hostilities, the Coalition's efforts in this area were still inadequate. A Human Rights Watch researcher found large unsecured ammunition stocks at the Second Military College north of Baghdad, including rooms filled with antitank mines, antipersonnel mines, mortars, and large stockpiles of multiple rocket launcher rocket heads. At the request of internally displaced persons living on the grounds, the researcher reported the stockpiles to U.S. military authorities in Baghdad, who promised immediate attention to the issue. For the next ten days, the researcher continued to report the find, yet the weapons remained unsecured, and the displaced persons reported that no U.S. military authorities had visited the college. It took nearly two weeks after the stockpile was

---

[411] Iraq Coalition Casualty Count, n.d., http://lunaville.org/warcasualties/Summary.aspx (retrieved November 11, 2003). As of November 11, 2003, this site listed a total of 281 Coalition military deaths after May 1, including 171 hostile and 110 non-hostile. From March 20 to May 1, it reported 172 deaths, including 142 hostile and 30 non-hostile.

initially reported for U.S. military authorities to send a response team. Despite the delays in some cases, U.S. forces recognized the need to attend to unguarded sites. In Karbala', Marine EOD team leader Gunnery Sergeant Tracey Jones said his team secured two "huge ammunition supply points" by building berms on four sides and blocking the doors.[412]

The British forces in Basra made little or no effort to secure the large sites near its posts in the city. The storage facility Human Rights Watch visited was about 600 meters (.4 miles) from the headquarters of the First Fusiliers Battle Group. According to a briefing by Lieutenant Colonel Alan Butterfield on May 3, the British had no plans to secure the sites because of a lack of manpower.[413] Human Rights Watch criticized this failure in a May 6 press release.[414] At the time, Basra's al-Jumhuriyya Hospital was receiving five victims a day from unsecured ordnance.[415] A month later, little had changed. The storage facility remained unsecured, and the U.K. forces were handing over clearance responsibility to UNMACT.

Iraqi looters have interfered with efforts to secure and clear sites. "If you put up extensive fencing, they just take it away," Lieutenant Colonel Shanahan said.[416] Instead his team resorted to waist high signs, twenty meters (sixty-five feet) apart, with red triangles. The looters also break open containers left secure by the Iraqi military. UNMACT's Van Ree said, on May 27, "[w]e walked away from [a cache near Basra] because the locals were ratting out [scattering] propellant while we were there."[417] The next day he visited a site with sixteen shipping containers of ammunition within 150 meters (.1 miles) of homes. "The problem in this case was that people broke open [the containers] and spread [the ammunition] around," he said.[418]

The Coalition's treatment of munitions caches also suffered from a shortage of clearance experts, but that should not have affected its ability to secure sites. A senior CENTCOM official said that many of its EOD teams had been in Afghanistan for a year and a half. "We tapped out every unit that was in existence. My assessment is it

---

[412] Human Rights Watch interview with Gunnery Sergeant Tracey Jones.

[413] Briefing by Lieutenant Colonel Alan Butterfield, British Army, CMOC, Basra, May 3, 2003.

[414] Human Rights Watch, "Iraq: Basra: Unprotected Munitions Injure Civilians," Press Release, May 6, 2003.

[415] Ibid.

[416] Human Rights Watch interview with Lieutenant Colonel John Shanahan.

[417] Human Rights Watch interview with Bill Van Ree, team leader, UNMACT, Basra, May 28, 2003.

[418] Human Rights Watch interview with Bill Van Ree, May 29, 2003.

was not enough," he said.[419] The Coalition, however, did not need specially trained EOD experts to secure sites. To speed up efforts, regular soldiers could provide security for abandoned munition caches.

Conclusion and Recommendations

By placing stockpiles of weapons and ammunition in civilian dwellings and schools and other protected locations, such as mosques and hospitals, Iraq rendered these otherwise protected sites potential military targets vulnerable to attack and put the local civilian population at risk.

This conduct violated various rules of international humanitarian law that aim to shield civilians from the effects of hostilities. These provisions include the rule on precautions that requires parties to a conflict "to the maximum extent feasible. . . avoid locating military objectives [such as stocks of weapons] within or near densely populated areas."[420] More specifically, IHL prohibits the use of places of worship, such as mosques, in support of the military effort, including by using them to store weapons.[421] Hospitals lose the protection from attack to which they are entitled if they are used to commit "acts harmful to the enemy."[422] Moreover, "medical units," which include hospitals, may not be used to "shield military objectives from attack."[423] While not explicitly illegal under international law, the placement of ordnance caches in schools and residential neighborhoods also increased the risk to civilians because they had greater access to the munitions once the military fled.

As occupying powers, the United States and United Kingdom have an obligation under international law to protect Iraqi civilians. According to Article 43 of the Hague Regulations, an occupying power "shall take all the measures in his power to restore, and ensure, as far as possible, public order and safety."[424] Abandoned munitions are currently one of the biggest threats to civilians. Looters and children endanger themselves and others when they break apart ordnance and spread the contents on the ground. Opposition forces have also used the explosives to launch attacks on civilians.

---

[419] Human Rights Watch interview with senior CENTCOM official #2.

[420] Protocol I, art. 58.

[421] Ibid., art. 53.

[422] Fourth Geneva Convention, art. 19.

[423] Protocol I, art. 12.

[424] Hague Regulations, art. 43.

To prevent further casualties and ensure public safety, the Coalition must secure remaining sites immediately and make sure they are cleared in the long run.

Although there is no existing treaty governing the handling of abandoned weapons caches, the States Parties to the Convention on Conventional Weapons (CCW) are negotiating a protocol on explosive remnants of war. The draft protocol reflects the international community's concern with unexploded ordnance and abandoned explosive ordnance.[425] It imposes duties on the state in control of the territory to clear and secure this ordnance. In the technical annex, it also encourages states that abandon ordnance to leave it "in a safe and secure manner."[426] This draft protocol is still under negotiation, but it lays down minimum standards for handling abandoned explosive ordnance, which have been largely unmet in Iraq. The Iraqis did not leave their caches secure, and the United States and United Kingdom did not take "all feasible precautions" to protect civilians when they failed to secure sites.[427]

Iraq and the United States and United Kingdom share responsibility for casualties caused by abandoned munition caches. Iraqi forces placed these caches in areas where civilians could potentially gain access and injure themselves. The United States and United Kingdom failed to secure the sites once they were in control of the territory. As a result, locals were injured or killed and clearance problems were exacerbated.

To address these issues in the future, Human Rights Watch recommends:

- Armed forces should avoid storing large caches of weapons and ammunition in populated areas and civilian buildings. Under no circumstances should caches be stored in hospitals or places of worship.

- Armed forces that expect to be in the position of occupying powers should do more pre-war planning for security of abandoned explosive ordnance.

---

[425] CCW, Draft Explosive Remnants of War Protocol, September 2003, art. 1(3).

[426] Ibid., Technical Annex.

[427] Ibid., art. 5.

APPENDICES

Appendix A: Civilian Casualties in al-Hilla

U.S. forces used cluster munitions extensively in and around al-Hilla. Dr. Sa`ad al-Falluji, director and chief surgeon of al-Hilla General Teaching Hospital, provided Human Rights Watch with copies of the hospital's records of civilian casualties due to combat in al-Hilla from March 23 to April 11, 2003. At the time, he was only able to provide numbers for casualties resulting from cluster munitions. These figures included casualties both during cluster munition strikes and from hazardous submunition duds after the strikes. Dr. al-Falluji said submunitions caused 90 percent of the injuries his hospital treated during the war.

Al-Hilla morgue provided some death records to Human Rights Watch. The director said that the morgue could not keep accurate records of the dead due to the pace of the war but estimated that the number was in the dozens.

Hospital and morgue records reported a total of 551 civilian casualties due to submunitions, including nineteen deaths, 515 injuries, and seventeen non-specified. Of the nineteen reported civilian deaths, fourteen were male and five were female. Eleven of the nineteen were children under the age of eighteen. Of the 515 reported injuries, 127 (25 percent) were children; 385 were male, 127 were female, and three did not have the sex recorded.

Fifteen civilian deaths and 171 injuries occurred on one day, March 31, as the U.S. Army pushed by al-Hilla on its way to Baghdad, according to al-Hilla hospital and morgue records. Nadir, an outlying district of al-Hilla, was particularly hard-hit by ground-launched submunitions. Hospital records show that 142 (28 percent) of the 515 injuries occurred in Nadir, including 109 on March 31. According to the *New York Times*, the strikes on Nadir killed thirty-three civilians on March 31.[428] Neighborhood elders in Nadir kept records that indicated that by September 2003, civilian casualties totaled 194 (thirty-eight dead and 156 injured) from both cluster strikes and cluster duds. Their documents listed 144 men, thirty-seven women, and thirteen whose sex could not be determined.

Dr. al-Falluji said that most of the 221 injuries recorded from April 1 to 11 were caused by submunition duds. Human Rights Watch researchers found predominantly U.S.

---

[428] Tyler Hicks and John F. Burns, "Iraq Shows Casualties in Hospital," *New York Times*, April 3, 2003.

ground-launched submunition duds in al-Hilla although there were a small number of duds from air-dropped cluster bombs as well. Post-war hospital records from May through August in al-Hilla list thirty-two injuries from submunition duds, including twenty-six male and six female.

Date	Total Civilian Injuries	Child Injuries	Total Civilian Deaths	Child Deaths	Total Civilian Casualties Unspecified	Child Casualties Unspecified
Unknown	-	-	1	-	17	4
3/23/03	9	3	-	-	-	-
3/24/03	10	3	-	-	-	-
3/25/03	52	9	-	-	-	-
3/26/03	7	3	-	-	-	-
3/27/03	26	-	-	-	-	-
3/28/03	6	2	-	-	-	-
3/29/03	3	1	-	-	-	-
3/30/03	10	2	-	-	-	-
3/31/03	171	48	15	11	-	-
4/1/03	24	8	-	-	-	-
4/2/03	15	4	-	-	-	-
4/3/03	12	7	1	-	-	-
4/4/03	71	14	2	-	-	-
4/5/03	13	1	-	-	-	-
4/6/03	6	2	-	-	-	-
4/7/03	13	3	-	-	-	-
4/8/03	24	5	-	-	-	-
4/9/03	39	9	-	-	-	-
4/10/03	3	2	-	-	-	-
4/11/03	1	1	-	-	-	-
Total	**515**	**127**	**19**	**11**	**17**	**4**

Note: Children are those under eighteen years of age.

Appendix B: Civilian Casualties in al-Najaf

Al-Najaf and its surrounding villages suffered hundreds of civilian casualties, most of which were caused by cluster munitions, according to medical professionals. Dr. Safa' al-`Amdi, director of al-Najaf Teaching Hospital, provided Human Rights Watch with copies of all of the hospital's records for civilian deaths and injuries attributed to combat in al-Najaf from March 21 to April 11, 2003.

- The hospital recorded 635 civilian casualties, including 254 deaths and 381 injuries.

- Of the 254 reported civilian deaths, 194 were male, fifty were female, and ten did not have the sex recorded.

- Of the civilian deaths, forty-seven (19 percent) were children under the age of eighteen.

- Of the 381 injuries, 263 were male, fifty-two were female, and sixty-six did not have the sex recorded.

- Eighty-one children (21 percent of the total) suffered injuries.

- Two hundred sixty-two (41 percent) of the civilian casualties occurred during the three days of fighting around al-Najaf from March 26 to 28.

In addition, a smaller, but unknown, number of civilian casualties was treated at al-Najaf General Hospital.

Date	Total Civilian Injuries	Child Injuries	Total Civilian Deaths	Child Deaths
Unknown	-	-	3	1
3/21/03	-	-	16	3
3/22/03	20	1	1	1
3/23/03	30	6	2	-
3/24/03	6	-	47	13
3/25/03	18	4	28	2
3/26/03	55	3	-	-
3/27/03	31	4	-	-
3/28/03	112	35	64	14
3/29/03	-	-	5	-
3/30/03	-	-	21	5
3/31/03	29	5	4	1
4/1/03	11	4	9	-
4/2/03	46	12	12	3
4/3/03	23	7	9	-
4/4/03	-	-	9	-
4/5/03	-	-	9	2
4/6/03	-	-	6	1
4/7/03	-	-	5	1
4/8/03	-	-	1	-
4/9/03	-	-	-	-
4/10/03	-	-	2	-
4/11/03	-	-	1	-
Total	**381**	**81**	**254**	**47**

Note: Children are those under eighteen years of age.

Appendix C: Civilian Deaths in al-Nasiriyya

Some of the deadliest fighting of the war occurred in al-Nasiriyya and resulted in more than 1,100 civilian casualties. The city suffered more civilian casualties than any other location in Iraq, except for Baghdad. Dr. `Ali `Abd al-Sayyid, director of al-Nasiriyya General Hospital, provided Human Rights Watch with copies of all the death certificates attributed to combat in al-Nasiriyya from March 20 to April 25, 2003. More than half of the civilian deaths occurred during the intense ground battle from March 23 to March 31, 2003.

The hospital reported that 405 civilians died, including 240 males, 162 females, and three with unrecorded sex. Of the deaths, 169 (42 percent) were children under the age of eighteen, including seventy-nine males and ninety females. Dr. `Abd al-Sayyid said that an additional 705 women and children suffered injuries.

Eighteen U.S. Marines were killed in the fighting in al-Nasiriyya. Thirty-five Iraqi soldiers and two fedayeen died in the hospital's care; more Iraqi troops likely died in the battle but were not brought to the hospital.

Date	Total Civilian Deaths	Child Deaths
Unknown	31	11
3/20/03	3	1
3/21/03	8	4
3/22/03	14	6
3/23/03	61	20
3/24/03	39	19
3/25/03	86	36
3/26/03	39	20
3/27/03	15	13
3/28/03	18	8
3/29/03	6	3
3/30/03	6	2
3/31/03	3	-
4/1/03	11	7
4/2/03	12	4
4/3/03	5	3
4/4/03	4	2
4/5/03	5	2
4/6/03	7	1
4/7/03	2	2
4/8/03	3	2
4/9/03	-	-
4/10/03	3	1
4/11/03	3	-
4/12-4/27/03	21	2
Total	**405**	**169**

Note: Children are those under eighteen years of age.

Appendix D: Weapons Used in the Air War[429]

Precision-Guided Munitions

Designation	Name or Nickname	Type	Number
BGM-109 *	Tomahawk Land Attack Missile (TLAM)	Cruise Missile	802
AGM-114	Hellfire	Laser-Guided Missile	562
AGM-130		Television- or Infrared-Guided Missile	4
AGM-65	Maverick	Television-, Infrared-, or Laser-Guided Missile	918
AGM-84	Stand Off Land Attack Missile-Extended Response (SLAM(ER))	Cruise Missile	3
AGM-86C/D	Conventional Air-Launched Cruise Missile (CALCM)	Cruise Missile	153
AGM-88	High Speed Anti-Radiation Missile (HARM)	Anti-Radar Missile	408
AGM-154 *	Joint Stand Off Weapon (JSOW)	GPS/Inertial Navigation System-Guided Glide Missile	253
EGBU-27	Penetrator	Laser- and GPS-Guided Missile (2,000 lb)	98
GBU-10	Paveway II	Laser-Guided Bomb (2,000 lb)	236
GBU-12	Paveway II	Laser-Guided Bomb (500 lb)	7,114
GBU-16	Paveway II	Laser-Guided Bomb (1,000 lb)	1,233
GBU-24	Paveway III	Laser-Guided Bomb (2,000 lb)	23
GBU-27	Penetrator	Laser-Guided Bomb (2,000 lb)	11
GBU-28	Bunker Buster	Laser-Guided Bomb (5,000 lb)	1

---

[429] The source for the types and numbers of air munitions expended used is Lt. Gen. T. Michael Moseley, U.S. Air Force, "Operation Iraqi Freedom—By The Numbers," April 30, 2003.

GBU-31	Joint Direct Attack Munition (JDAM)	GPS-Guided Bomb (2,000 lb)	5,086
GBU-32	JDAM	GPS-Guided Bomb (1,000 lb)	768
GBU-35	JDAM	GPS-Guided Bomb (1,000 lb)	675
GBU-37	JDAM	GPS-Guided Bomb (5,000 lb)	13
Various	U.K. Guided Munitions		679
Total			**19,040**

* These weapons can deliver a unitary warhead or submunitions, but the U.S. Air Force has not indicated how many of each type were used.

Unguided Unitary Munitions

Designation	Type	Number
M117	General Purpose Bomb (750 lb)	1,625
Mk-82	General Purpose Bomb (500 lb)	5,504
Mk-83	General Purpose Bomb (1,000 lb)	1,692
Mk-84	General Purpose Bomb (2,000 lb)	6
Various	U.K. General Purpose Bombs	58
Total		**8,885**

Cluster Bombs

Designation	Name	Guidance	Number	Submunitions per Weapon	Total Submunitions
CBU-87		Unguided	118	202	23,836
CBU-99	Rockeye	Unguided	182	247	44,954
CBU-103		WCMD	818	202	165,236
CBU-105	Sensor Fuzed Weapon	WCMD, Infrared	88	40 (10 submunitions with 4 skeets)	3,520
CBU-107*	Passive Attack Weapon System	WCMD			Non-explosive
UK RBL-755		Unguided	70	147	10,290
Total**			1,276		247,836

* The CBU-107 has a non-explosive payload of 3,700 metal rods.

** It is not known how many JSOW and TLAM missiles carried submunitions.

Aircraft

Aircraft	Number	Sorties
Fighters	735	20,228
Bombers	51	505
Other	1,015	20,671
Total	1,801	41,404

Note: "Fighter" aircraft carry bombs and engage in bombing missions. "Other" includes aircraft for refueling; airlifts; command and control; intelligence, surveillance, and reconnaissance; rescue; and more.

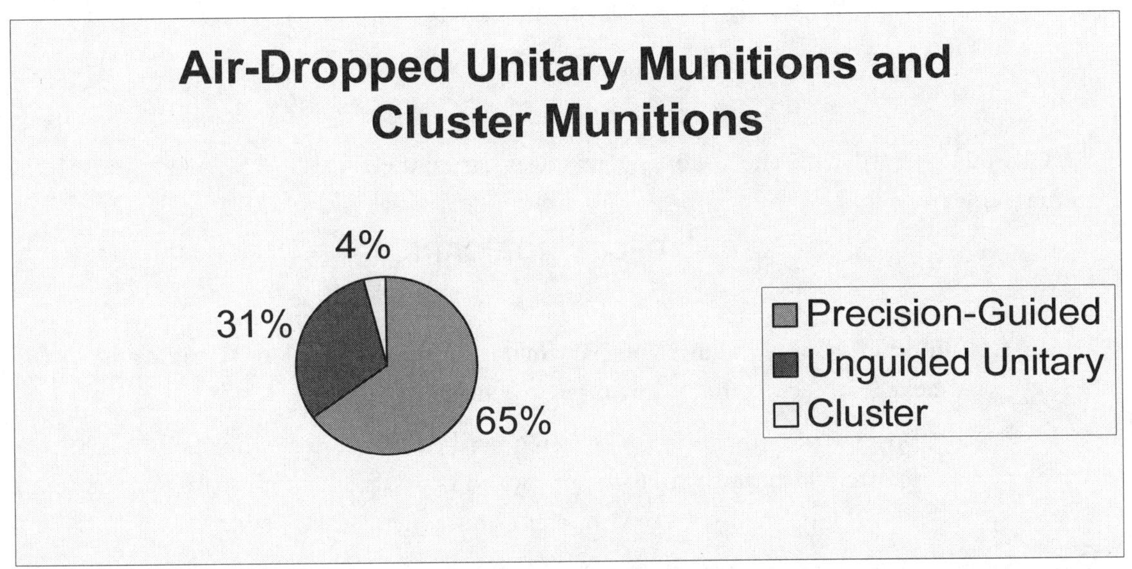

Air-Dropped Unitary Munitions and Cluster Munitions
4%
31%
65%
Precision-Guided
Unguided Unitary
Cluster

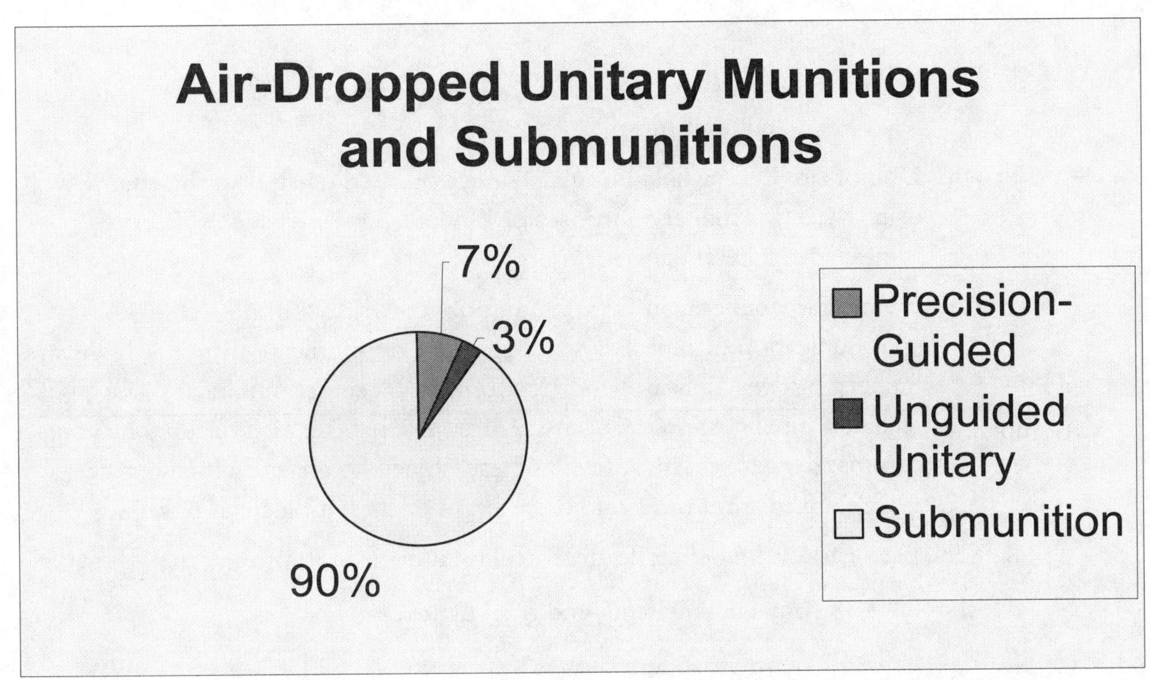

Air-Dropped Unitary Munitions and Submunitions
7%
3%
90%
Precision-Guided
Unguided Unitary
Submunition

Appendix E: Rules of Engagement for U.S. Military Forces in Iraq
Issued by U.S. Central Command Combined Forces Land Component
Commander

A laminated card with the following text was distributed to all U.S. Army and Marine personnel in Iraq.

CFLCC ROE CARD

1. On order, enemy military and paramilitary forces are declared hostile and may be attacked subject to the following instructions:

   a) Positive identification (PID) is required prior to engagement. PID is a reasonable certainty that the proposed target is a legitimate military target. If no PID, contact your next higher commander for decision

   b) Do not engage anyone who has surrendered or is out of battle due to sickness or wounds.

   c) Do not target or strike any of the following except in self-defense to protect yourself, your unit, friendly forces, and designated persons or property under your control:

      - Civilians

      - Hospitals, mosques, national monuments, and any other historical and cultural sites.

   d) Do not fire into civilian populated areas or buildings unless the enemy is using them for military purposes or if necessary for your self-defense. Minimize collateral damage.

   e) Do not target enemy infrastructure (public works, commercial communication facilities, dams), Lines of Communication (roads, highways, tunnels, bridges, railways) and Economic Objects (commercial storage facilities, pipelines) unless necessary for self-defense or if ordered by your commander. If you must fire on these objects to engage a hostile force, disable and disrupt but avoid destruction of these objects, if possible.

2. The use of force, including deadly force, is authorized to protect the following:

   - Yourself, your unit, and friendly forces

   - Enemy Prisoners of War

- Civilians from crimes that are likely to cause death or serious bodily harm, such as murder or rape
- Designated civilians and/or property, such as personnel of the Red Cross/Crescent, UN, and US/UN supported organizations

3. Treat all civilians and their property with respect and dignity. Do not seize civilian property, including vehicles, unless you have the permission of a company level commander and you give a receipt to the property's owner.

4. Detain civilians if they interfere with mission accomplishment or if required for self-defense.

5. CENTCOM General Order No. 1A remains in effect. Looting and the taking of war trophies are prohibited.

REMEMBER

- Attack enemy forces and military targets.
- Spare civilians and civilian property, if possible.
- Conduct yourself with dignity and honor.
- Comply with the Law of War. If you see a violation, report it.

These ROE will remain in effect until your commander orders you to transition to post-hostilities ROE.

AS OF 311330Z JAN 03

Appendix F: Maps

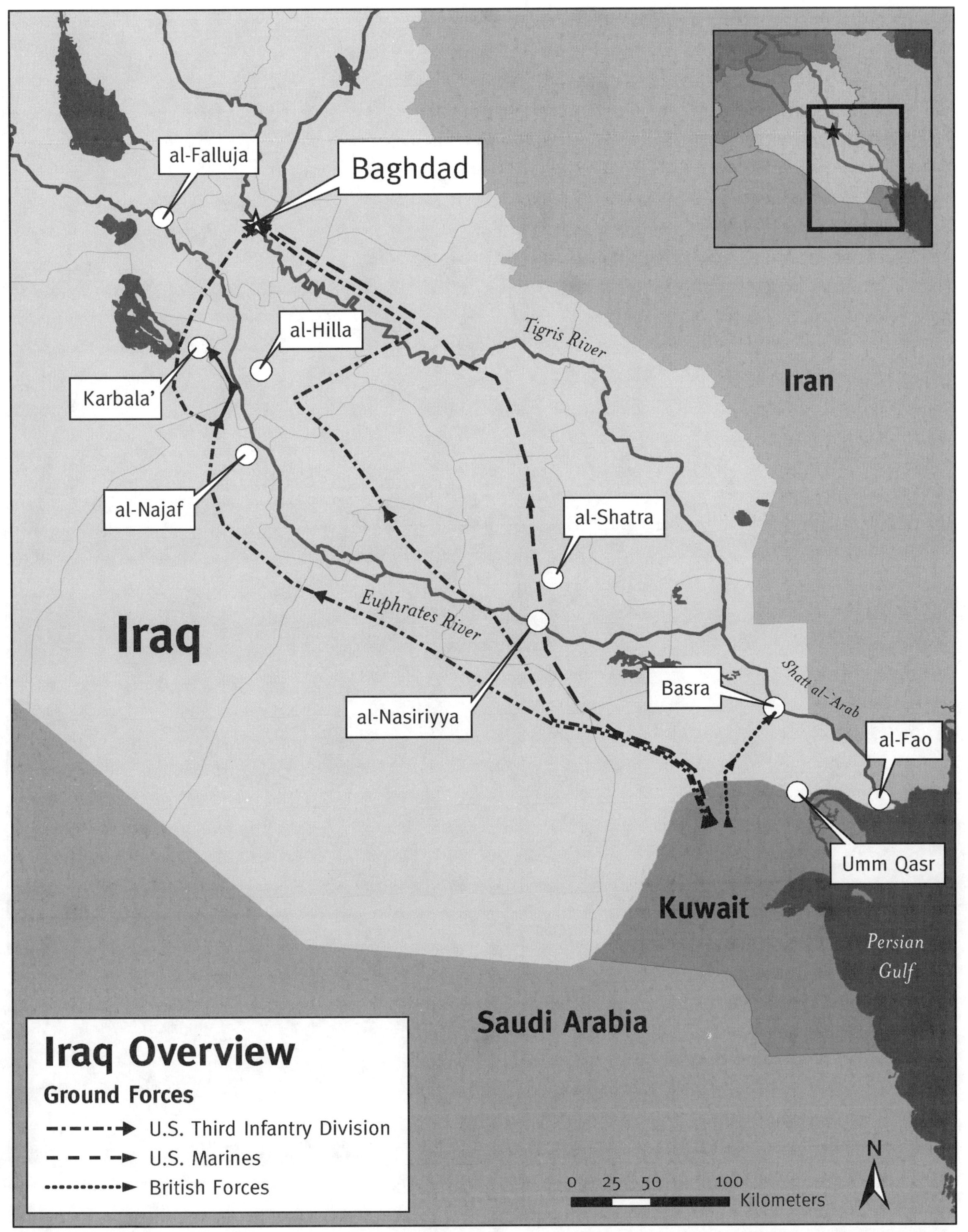

Map Source: "Baghdad," U.S. National Imagery and Mapping Agency (NIMA), Special Reference Graphic, 2003 (obtained from NIMA at http://www.nima.mil/)

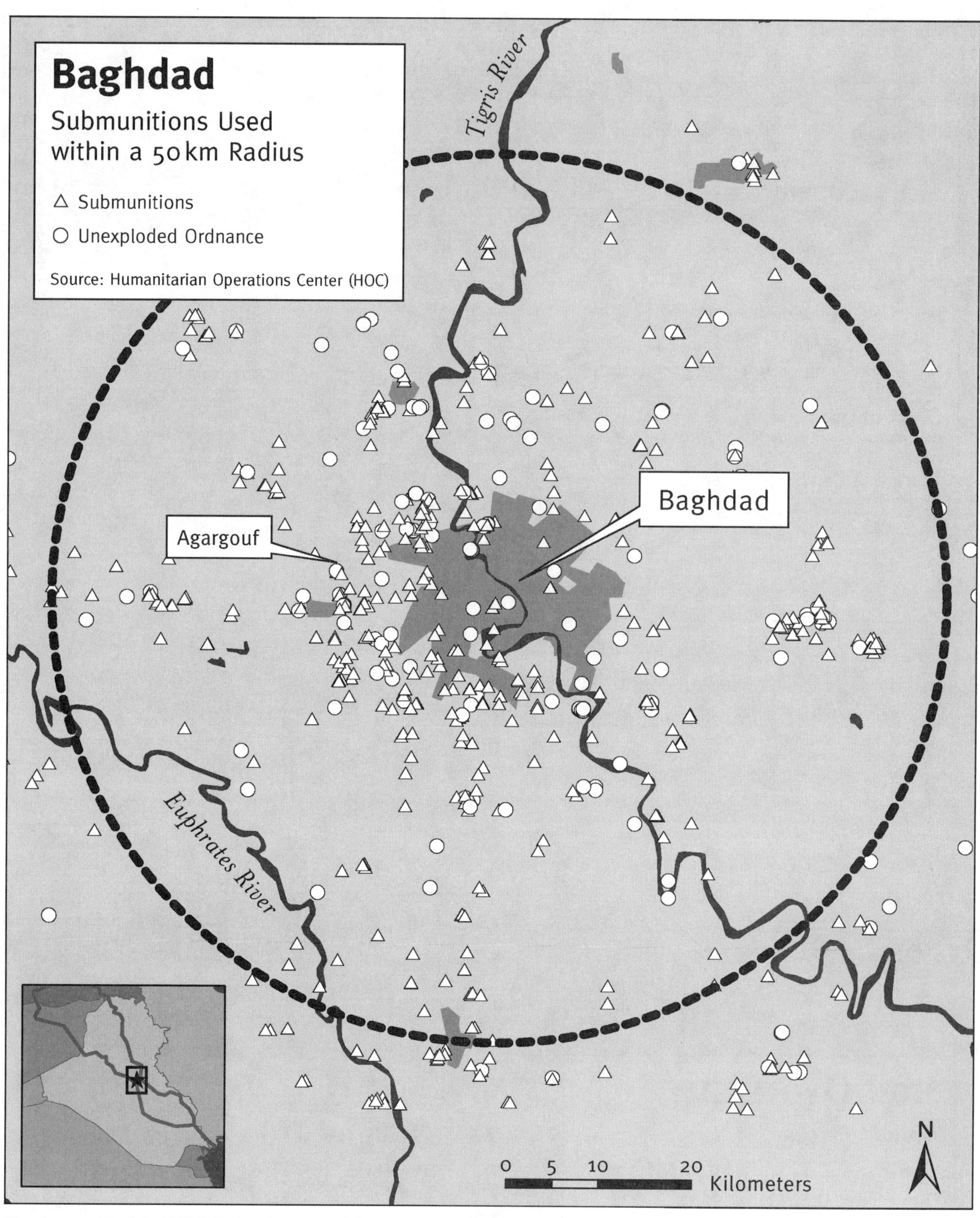

Map Source: "Baghdad," U.S. National Imagery and Mapping Agency (NIMA), Special Reference Graphic, 2003 (obtained from NIMA at http://www.nima.mil/)

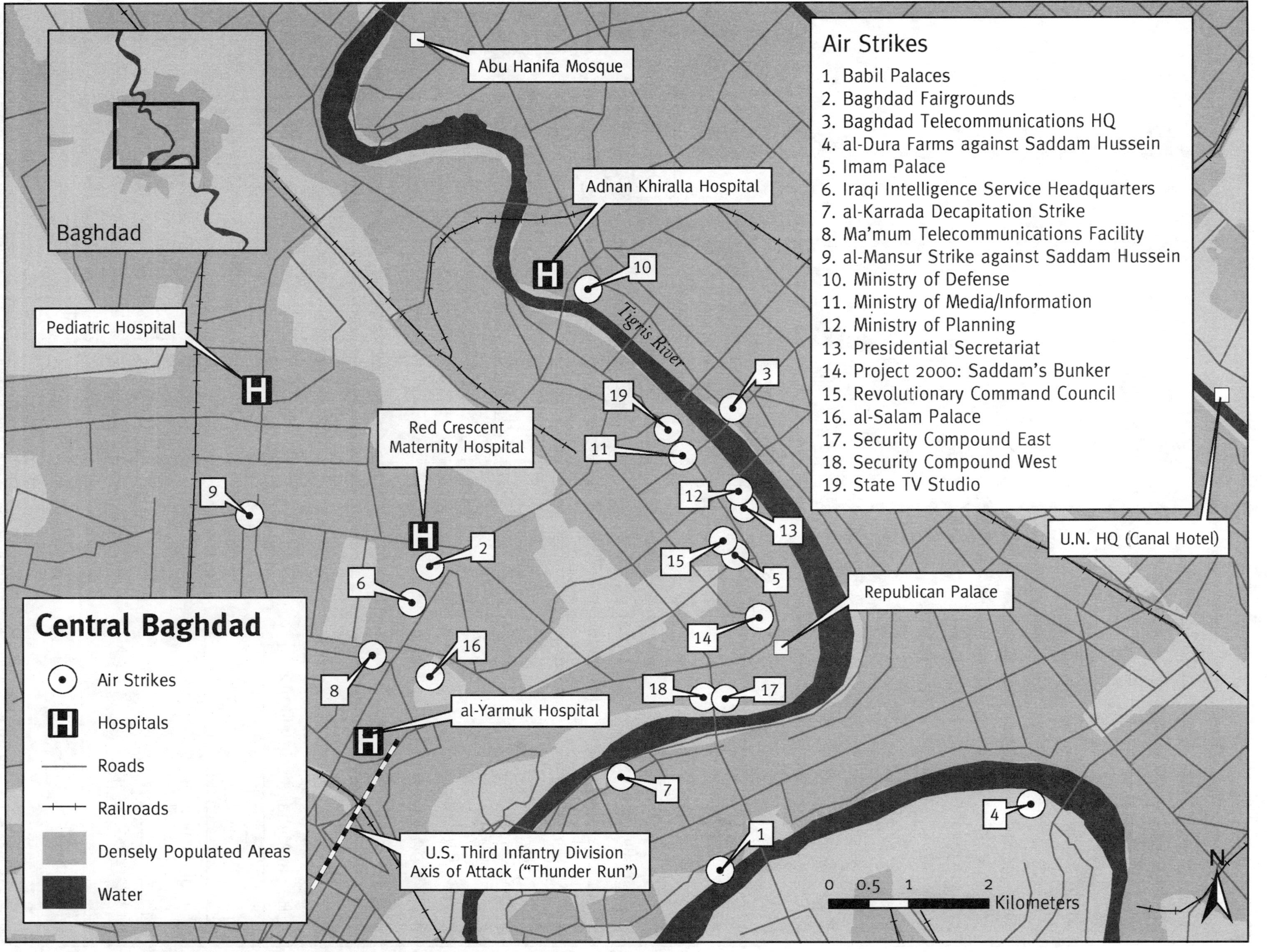

Map Source: "Baghdad," U.S. National Imagery and Mapping Agency (NIMA), Special Reference Graphic, 2003 (obtained from NIMA at http://www.nima.mil/)

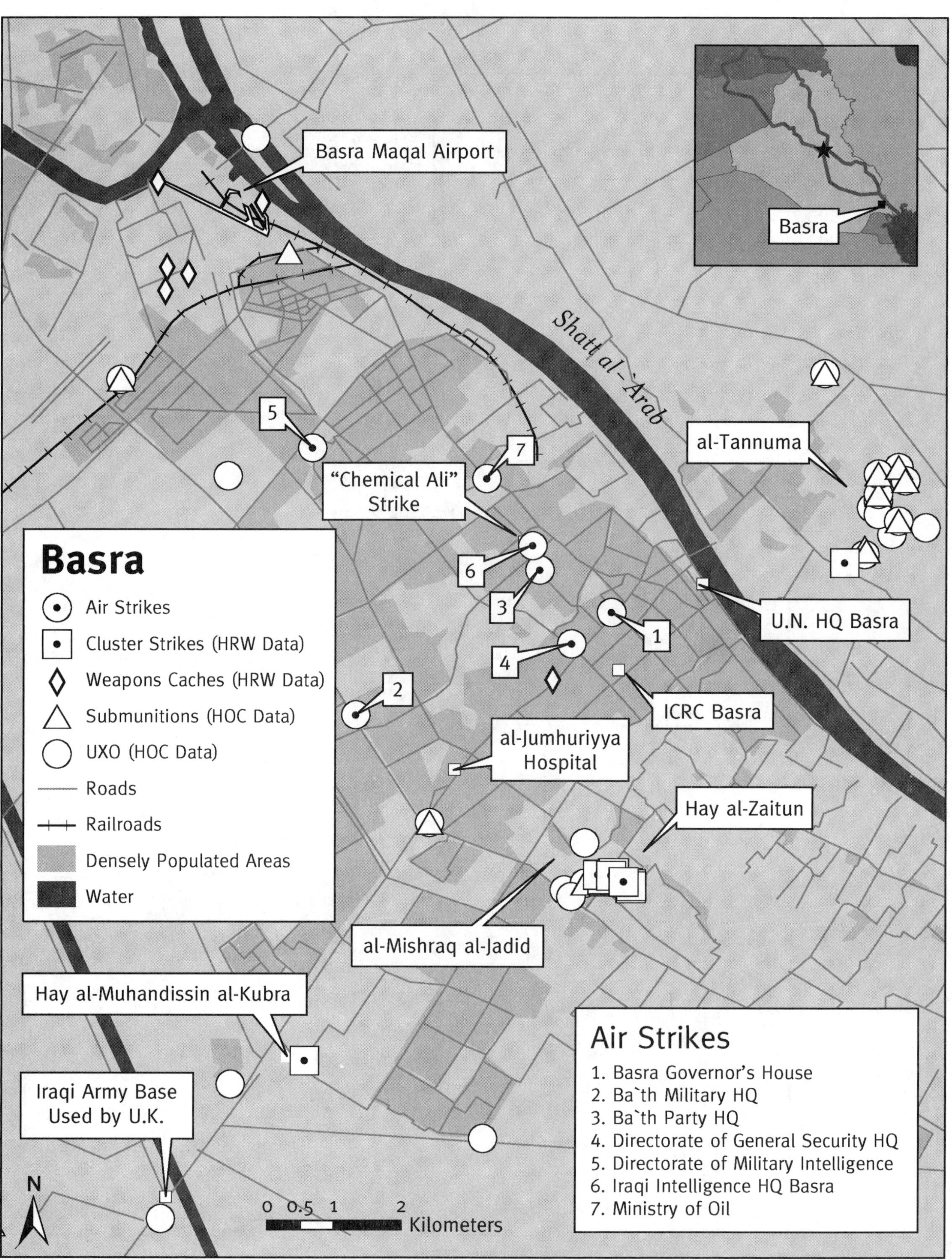

Map Source: "Al Basrah, Iraq," U.S. National Imagery and Mapping Agency (NIMA), April 24, 2003 (obtained from the Humanitarian Information Center at http://www.hiciraq.org/default.asp)

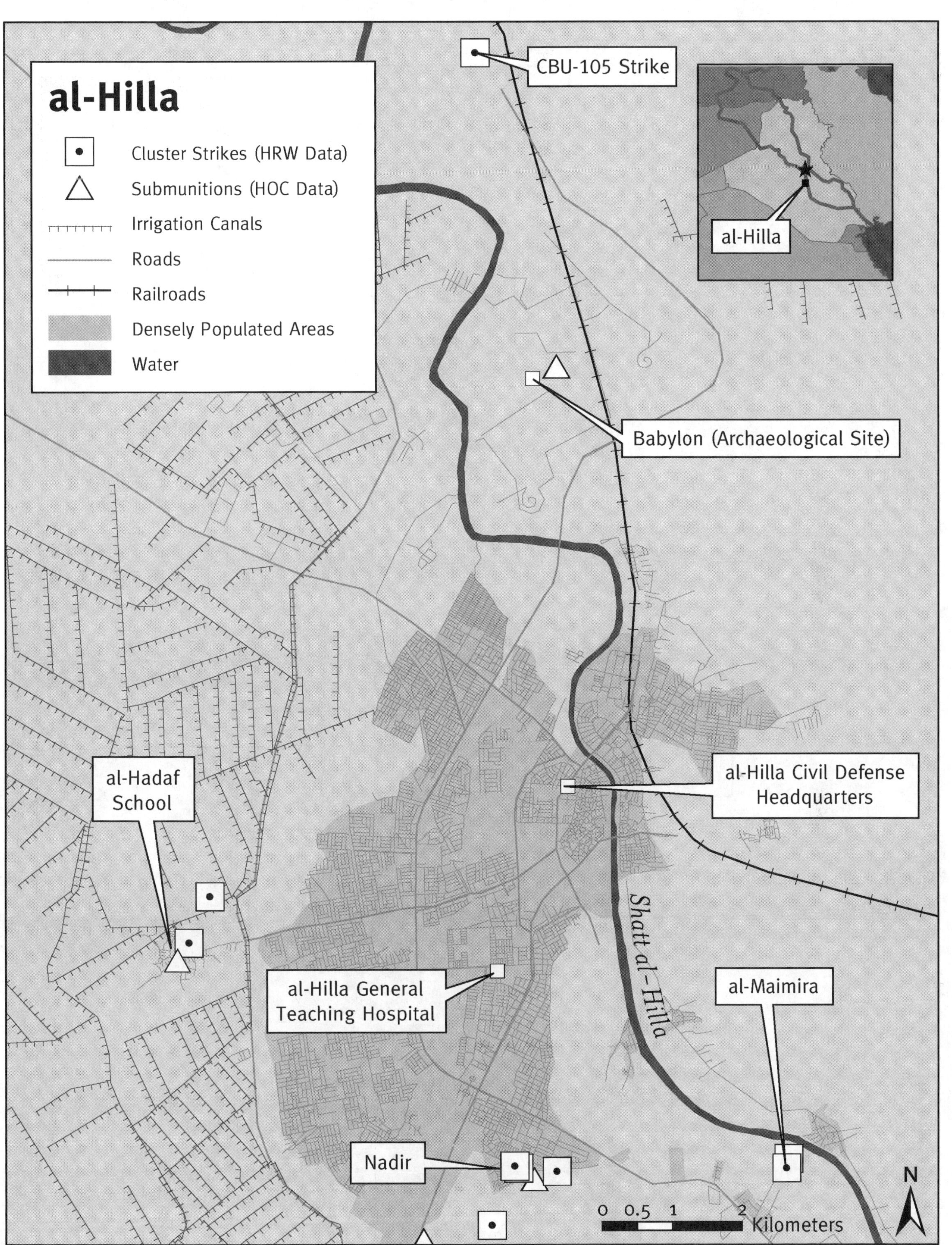

Map Source: "City of Hilla," Humanitarian Information Center, Map HIC Reference 334 (obtained from the Humanitarian Information Center at http://www.hiciraq.org/default.asp) and SpaceImaging.com

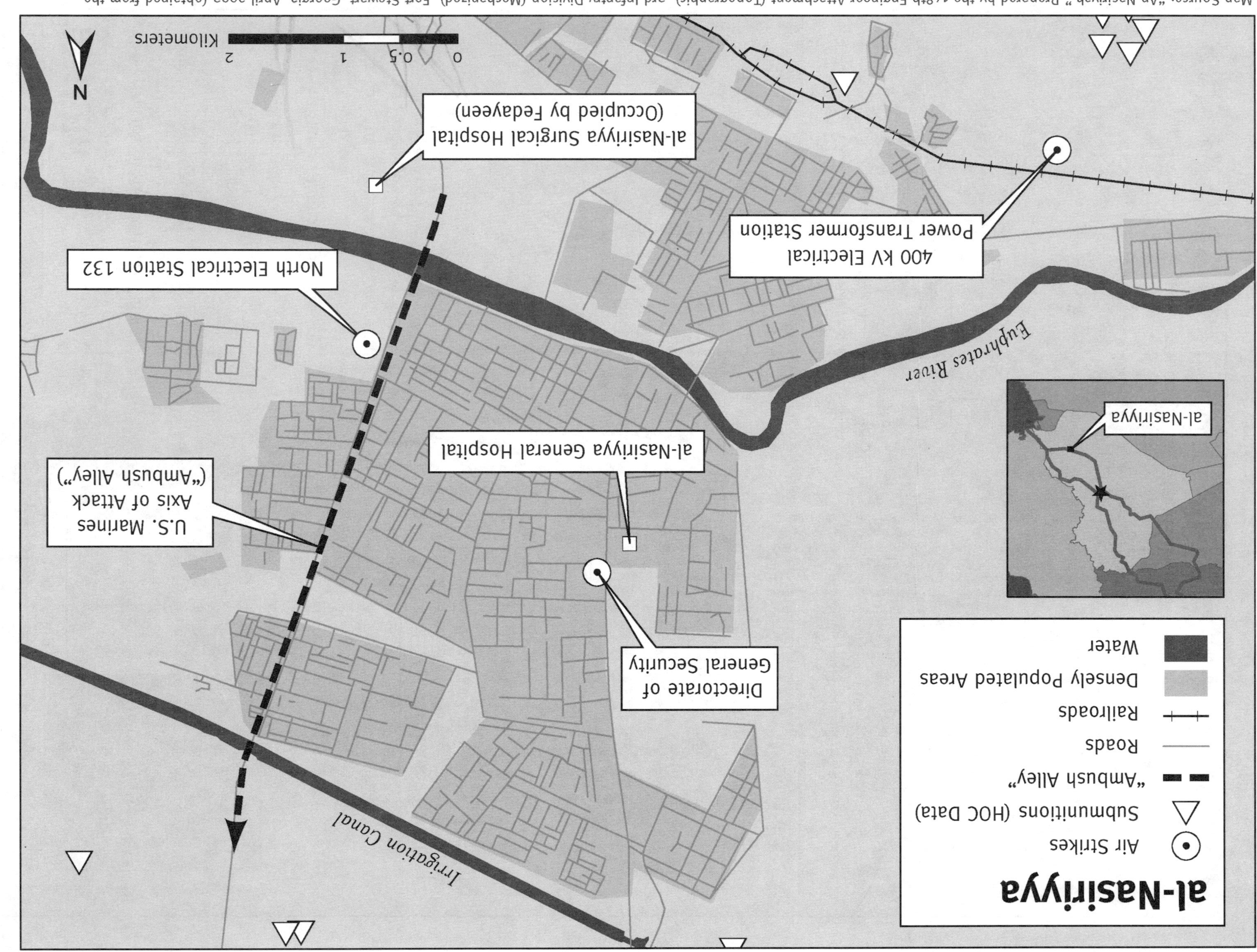

Map Source: "An Nasiriyah," Prepared by the 148th Engineer Attachment (Topographic), 3rd Infantry Division (Mechanized), Fort Stewart, Georgia, April 2003 (obtained from the Humanitarian Information Center at http://www.hiciraq.org/default.asp) and Spaceimaging.com

ACKNOWLEDGEMENTS

This report was written by Bonnie Docherty, researcher, and Marc E. Garlasco, senior military analyst, both in the Arms Division of Human Rights Watch. Field research was conducted by Reuben E. Brigety, II, then researcher in the Arms Division, Bonnie Docherty, and Marc E. Garlasco. Olivier Bercault, counsel, Peter Bouckaert, senior emergencies researcher, Sasha Petrov, deputy director of the Europe and Central Asia Division, and Sam Zia-Zarifi, deputy director of the Asia Division, provided research and logistical support. `Abd al-Razzaq al-Sa`idi, consultant for the Arms Division, provided additional research. The report was reviewed and edited by Stephen Goose, executive director of the Arms Division, Iain Levine, program director of Human Rights Watch, James Ross, senior legal advisor of Human Rights Watch, and Wilder Tayler, legal and policy director of Human Rights Watch. Matthew Klag, research assistant for the Arms Division, and Najiyah Alwazir, Nesma Farahat, and Brian Truss, interns for the Arms Division, provided research and translation assistance. Mohamed Abdel Dayem, associate with the Middle East and North Africa Division, provided transliteration services. Jamila Homayun and Carly Tubbs, associates with the Arms Division, provided research and production assistance. John Emerson, web advocate for Human Rights Watch, provided assistance with the maps and satellite images. Veronica Matushaj, photo editor and associate director of Creative Services for Human Rights Watch, provided assistance with the photographs. Andrea Holley, publications director for Human Rights Watch, and Fitzroy Hepkins, mail manager, made possible the production of this report.

We owe special thanks to Matthew McKinzie of the Natural Resources Defense Council, who produced the maps in this report for Human Rights Watch, and Space Imaging, which provided the satellite images.

Human Rights Watch would also like to thank all the individuals in Iraq, the United States, and United Kingdom who provided information or testimony for this report, and in particular the medical community of Iraq for open access to hospital records and for facilitating visits with civilian victims. Additional thanks go to Marla Ruzicka of CIVIC and the U.N. Mine Action Coordination Team.

Finally, Human Rights Watch would like to express its appreciation for the financial support of the ACT Netherlands, Ruth McLean Bowers Foundation, J.M. Kaplan Fund, John D. and Catherine T. MacArthur Foundation, Stichting Novib, Oak Foundation, Overbrook Foundation, David and Lucile Packard Foundation, Rockefeller Brothers Fund, David Brown, co-chair of the Arms Division Advisory Committee, and the many individuals who contributed to Human Rights Watch's Iraq emergency fund.